CARE IN THE COMMUNITY: FIVE YEARS ON

LIFE IN THE COMMUNITY FOR PEOPLE WITH LEARNING DISABILITIES

The Joseph Rowntree Foundation has supported this project as part of its programme of research and innovative development projects, which it hopes will be of value to policy makers and practitioners. The facts presented and the views expressed in this report, however, are those of the authors and not necessarily those of the Foundation.

Care in the Community: Five Years On

Life in the Community for People with Learning Disabilities

Paul Cambridge, Lesley Hayes and Martin Knapp with Eriko Gould and Andrew Fenyo

arena

First published in Great Britain in 1994

Arena
Ashgate Publishing Ltd
Gower House
Croft Road
Aldershot
Hants GU11 3HR
England

Ashgate Publishing Company
Old Post Road
Brookfield
Vermont
U.S.A.

British Library Cataloguing in Publication Data
Cambridge, P.
    Care in the Community: Five Years On — Life in the Community for
    People with Learning Disabilities
    I. Title
    362.10425
ISBN 1-85742-275-9 (pbk)
    1-85742-282-1 (hbk)

Library of Congress Cataloging-in-Publication Data
Care in the community--five years on: life in the community for
  people with learning disabilities / Paul Cambridge ... [et al.].
    p. cm.
  "PSSRU, University of Kent at Canterbury."
  Includes bibliographical references and indexes.
  ISBN 1-85742-275-9: $25.00 (approx.) (pbk)
  ISBN 1-85742-282-1: $49.95 (approx.) (hbk)
    1. Mentally handicapped--Care--Great Britain. 2. Learning
  disabled--Care--Great Britain. 3. Community mental health services-
  -Great Britain. I. Cambridge, Paul, 1952-   . II. University of
  Kent at Canterbury. Personal Social Services Research Unit.
  HV3008.G7C36 1994
  362.1'9685889'00941--DC20   94-28012
                                                                   CIP

Typeset by Jane Dennett at the PSSRU, University of Kent at Canterbury
Printed and bound in Great Britain by Hartnolls Ltd, Bodmin, Cornwall

Contents

vi

Figures

Acknowledgements

This research was conducted when the authors were all members of the Personal Social Services Research Unit (PSSRU), University of Kent at Canterbury. Paul Cambridge is now Lecturer and Service Development Consultant, Tizard Centre, University of Kent at Canterbury. Lesley Hayes is Research Associate, Hester Adrian Research Centre, University of Manchester. Martin Knapp is Professor of the Economics of Social Care, PSSRU, and also Professor of Health Economics and Director, Centre for the Economics of Mental Health, Institute of Psychiatry, London. Eriko Gould is now based at the University of Botswana. Andrew Fenyo is Senior Computing Officer, PSSRU.

The research would not have been possible without the considerable cooperation and indulgence of service users and staff in the twelve areas covered by our research. Denise Largin helped produce the account of CSMH at a time when she and the organisation were under great pressure. We also thank our PSSRU colleagues Jeni Beecham and Steve Carter for assistance, and the project's Advisory Group, particularly Nancy Korman, Ken Simons and Linda Ward, for advice at key stages in the research. Lesley Banks, Maureen Weir, Sarah Conyer and Glenys Harrison provided secretarial support of the highest standard and greatest patience, and Jane Dennett sub-edited the text. The Joseph Rowntree Foundation generously supported this project, but the material presented here represents the findings of the authors, not necessarily those of the Foundation.

1 Introduction

Long-term care in hospital for people with learning disabilities may eventually be a thing of the past. Across the country, agencies and individuals are working to create and maintain supportive community care services. Health and local authorities, voluntary and private sector agencies, families and other carers are all contributing to important developments in community care, and many service users are actively planning and reframing their lives both individually and collectively.

There remain challenges. One is the task of providing the community care and support needed by people who have spent long periods in hospital — perhaps all or most of their lives. According to government figures there were 16,000 people resident in hospital under the learning disability (mental handicap) specialty in England on 31 March 1993. Two-thirds of these people had been in continuous residence in the same hospital for three years or more. For some of these people, an isolated institutional life is all they know, and moving to the community brings enormous anxieties and risks as well as opportunities and the potential for individual development and change.

How successful is this policy of 'dehospitalisation'? How well have former hospital residents adjusted to their new lives in the community? How have community care agencies responded to their needs and preferences? These were the core questions which we addressed in a major research study supported by the Joseph Rowntree Foundation and undertaken at the Personal Social Services Research Unit at the University of Kent at Canterbury.

Research aims

We looked at key aspects of the lives of more than 200 people with learning disabilities who left long-stay hospital for the community in the mid-1980s. These people had been included in an earlier evaluation of community care, moving from hospital under the auspices of the (then) Department of Health and Social Security's Care in the Community demonstration programme. The programme and its effects on the lives of former hospital residents in their first year in the community, as well as its organisational, staffing and cost implications, have been reported previously (Renshaw et al., 1988; Knapp et al., 1992). Twelve social services authorities, twelve district health authorities and a number of voluntary organisations were involved in planning and providing the services and support for the people with learning disabilities. A few former hospital residents lived independently in their own flats, although most received specialist learning disability services.

Our earlier research allowed us to interview most people before they moved from hospital to the community, and again nine to twelve months later. Then, as now, we were keen to gain users' own views of their lives, aspirations and concerns. Support staff in hospital and the community were also interviewed to supplement the individual pictures of users, the services provided and the local organisational and resource contexts.

This book is concerned with the *longer*-term circumstances of life in the community. We have interviewed users and staff five years after the move from hospital, again looking at accommodation and quality of life, service use and costs, care management and strategic organisation. In this book we therefore describe the lives of these people after a longer period in the community, making comparisons with the situation a year after leaving hospital and prior to leaving hospital. We shall see that there was little change in individual skills and accomplishments between one and five years. There were some modest improvements, but the general message was the successful maintenance of skills acquired in the early months after leaving hospital. For the group as a whole, there were also few changes in aspects of behaviour, social networks and integration into ordinary life. However, some people were continuing to develop confidence, further competence and a range of skills, while some others were showing signs of deterioration in their abilities and quality of life.

An important component of the research was the series of interviews with the former hospital residents involved in the study. We shall therefore report their own views about their lives and the support they receive. By using both structured and semi-structured approaches, the interviews gave us revealing insights into community care from those directly affected by it. While certainly not a participative study — the work being researcher-led — we nevertheless sought the informed consent of users, and developed techniques to facilitate their participation.

The interviews with former hospital residents and those with carers also asked about the services people used and the services they would have liked, allowing us to summarise ones identified by carers or care managers as necessary but not currently available. For those services used, costs can also be attached. The costs of community care were compared with the earlier costs of supporting these people in the community and in hospital. Costs were also compared at five years *across* the sample, and were examined in the context of changes in quality of life and users' needs. These findings tell us a lot about the patterns of community care, the consequences of service packages for individual people, and the cost-effectiveness of different types of community-based support. This examination of the links between costs, needs and individual quality of life, and any changes over time, was one of the primary objectives of the research.

A final strand of our research was the description of the local organisation of community care for people with learning disabilities. We looked at the strategic (or macro) organisation and the tactical (micro or care management) arrangement of community care, including some of the planning, purchasing and providing implications within the mixed economy of care now developing rapidly in all areas of the country. Once again, our research design allowed us to chart some of the changes over a five-year period, and we highlight some of the organisational successes and failures of community care in the twelve former 'projects' to which the people participating in our study had moved.

Structure of the book

In the following chapter we introduce the policy and practice backgrounds to the services included in the research, and describe the original aims of the pilot projects funded under the Care in the Community demonstration programme in the mid-1980s. Chapter 3 outlines the methodological framework for our evaluation. Chapter 4 examines the broad service principles and practices adopted in the twelve areas and describes community accommodation. The next chapter looks at staffing.

We then turn to user quality of life and outcomes, the latter defined as changes in individual quality of life over time. We were particularly interested in the impact of community care on skills and accomplishments, behaviour, social networks, morale and life satisfaction (Chapter 6). Services and associated costs are covered in Chapter 7. The organisation and management of community care are the subject of Chapter 8, and the next chapter focuses on care management. Finally, we draw conclusions from our research about the successes and failures of community care for people with learning disabilities who have moved out of hospital.

2 Policy and Practice Backgrounds

The national policy context

The number of people with learning disabilities in National Health Service hospitals in England has more than halved since 1979. Over the ten-year period up to 1993, the average rate of decline was as high as 9 per cent each year. Numerous hospitals closed. The rundown of the large Victorian 'mental handicap hospitals' has been government policy for many decades, but it is clearly not the government's intention that they should be replaced by wards in general hospitals or by neglect in the community. Rather, local authorities are encouraged to coordinate the work of public sector and other agencies to offer comprehensive community care which is responsive to the needs of users and carers.

The White Paper, *Caring for People* (Secretaries for State, 1989) and the 1990 National Health Service and Community Care Act which followed it offer a new framework and a refocused set of objectives to take community care forward into the next century. The central elements of the community care reforms heralded by *Caring for People* and introduced in the 1990 Act are now well known. At the core is a restatement of the government's commitment to care in the community, especially in domiciliary settings with appropriate peripatetic support, in preference to long-stay residence in hospital, residential care homes or nursing homes. Supply pluralism is strongly encouraged by the community care reforms. A mixed economy of provision is developing quite rapidly in many areas, with local authorities taking the lead as 'enabling or managing agents' to purchase services from a range of providers. New forms of provision are expected to emerge with local authority encouragement and financial support, particularly within the voluntary and private sectors. Market forces are already exerting a much greater influence on future service and placement decisions. Purchasing strategies and provider competition will certainly shape community care over the coming years.

There has also been some realignment of the balance of responsibilities between the National Health Service, the Department of Social Security and local government. In particular, the reforms introduced by the 1990 Act give lead responsibility to local authorities for coordinating services for people with learning disabilities. Much of the funding formerly routed to private and voluntary homes via social security payments has been transferred to local authorities. The major public sector players in each locality must agree an annual plan for community care in consultation with the non-statutory sectors, users and carers. Fundamental to these changes is the movement away from allocations of services to individuals dominated by what services happen to be available, towards allocations which respond to needs which have been carefully and consistently assessed. The new arrangements should, where possible, be needs-led — capable of responding flexibly to the assessed needs of individuals — and should give more prominence to the views and preferences of service users, their carers, and others who support them.

The central aims of these reforms — community-based care, a mixed economy and the development of needs-led services — have been government policy since the early 1980s. In fact, the emphasis on community care in preference to hospital has been national policy for much longer. The difference is that the debates of the late 1980s and the implementation challenges of the 1990s have given community care policy, both centrally and locally, the potential for greater clarity, coherence, internal consistency in design and greater comprehensiveness in coverage. The reality has yet to measure up to these ideals, but the organisation, funding and delivery of community care are already changing markedly (Wistow et al., 1994).

In the mid-1980s, some of the Care in the Community pilot projects were already exploring one of the strategic options for organising and funding community care which had been identified, for example, by the influential Audit Commission report of 1986, namely local authority responsibility for long-term care. Some had already begun to pool health and social services budgets, even if only for the demonstration project itself over the three-year pilot period. Some had appointed a single manager and/or committee to coordinate and sometimes also purchase services. At the next organisational tier down, integrated service management and planning across agencies (sometimes both statutory and voluntary) were features of a few projects. User-centred services were a core objective, particularly in projects which introduced devolved decision-making, some form of care management and/ or advocacy programmes (compare Audit Commission, 1987).

The projects upon which our research focuses were established in the mid-1980s, and some were clearly seen as local torch-bearers. Each evolved in important ways during a decade of almost unprecedented community care attention, policy debate and change. Their early status as innovative pilot services provided experiential lessons for the management and organisation of community care, which in turn had some influence on the direction of central government policy discussions. For example, the Audit Commission (1989) referenced the design of, and the opportunities and difficulties encountered by, the Maidstone project and of the demonstration programme more generally. Sir Roy Griffiths visited a number of the projects, and the recommendations in his 1988 report built upon some of their experiences. After the passage of the 1990 *NHS and Community Care Act*, central government guidance also reflected lessons learned from the early years of the demonstration programme. For instance, in *Care Management and Assessment: Manager's Guide* (DH/SSI, 1991a) policy advisers identified exactly those models of interagency planning and care management distinguished within the programme (Knapp et al., 1992, Chap. 10; Cambridge, 1992b).

We can therefore see that the projects which provided the local frameworks within which more than 200 people with learning disabilities could move from hospital were both influenced by, and directly influenced, national as well as local developments in community care policy and practice between the mid-1980s and early 1990s. In today's terminology, they helped to bridge the implementation gap between central policy intentions and local service management and design. Most of them, as we shall report below, also functioned as catalysts for local change.

The Care in the Community programme

The events which precipitated our research were the moves of a number of people with learning disabilities from hospital into the community. These moves were first mooted in the early 1980s in the government's Care in the Community initiative. It was never intended by the Department of Health and Social Security (as it then was), or the health and local authorities and the non-statutory bodies who jointly implemented the pilot services, that these moves should be seen *simply* as relocations of care for a group of vulnerable people. No matter how challenging these moves would be to the people experiencing them, or however promising to the people campaigning for better services and opportunities for people with learning disabilities, the relocation from hospital was as opportunity to improve individual quality of life and also an opportunity to test the feasibility and quality of community care under carefully monitored circumstances (with in-built safeguards to minimise risks to individuals and agencies).

It was intended that both good and bad experiences from the pilot services were to be disseminated. The projects which secured special DHSS pump-priming grants shared a commitment to carefully coordinated, needs-led care planning. Each sought to shift the locus of care from hospital to community, in turn requiring changes to the balance of funding and provision between local government and the health service. Improved coordination of service responses to individual needs was a further component of the demonstration programme.

The Care in the Community programme did not lay down a single model of community care. One result was that many different routes, services and 'care technologies' were developed to help long-stay residents and resources move from hospital and sustain them in the community. Most moves were well planned.

Grants totalling more than £26 million (at 1994 prices) supported 28 projects spread across England, each funded for three years between 1984 and 1989, and each supplemented with local resources. Twelve of the projects supported people with learning disabilities, one of them for young people who also had physical disabilities (Figure 2.1). The other projects supported people with mental health problems, physical disabilities or age-related needs. The programme helped more than 900 individuals move from hospital over a three-

Figure 2.1
Care in the Community map

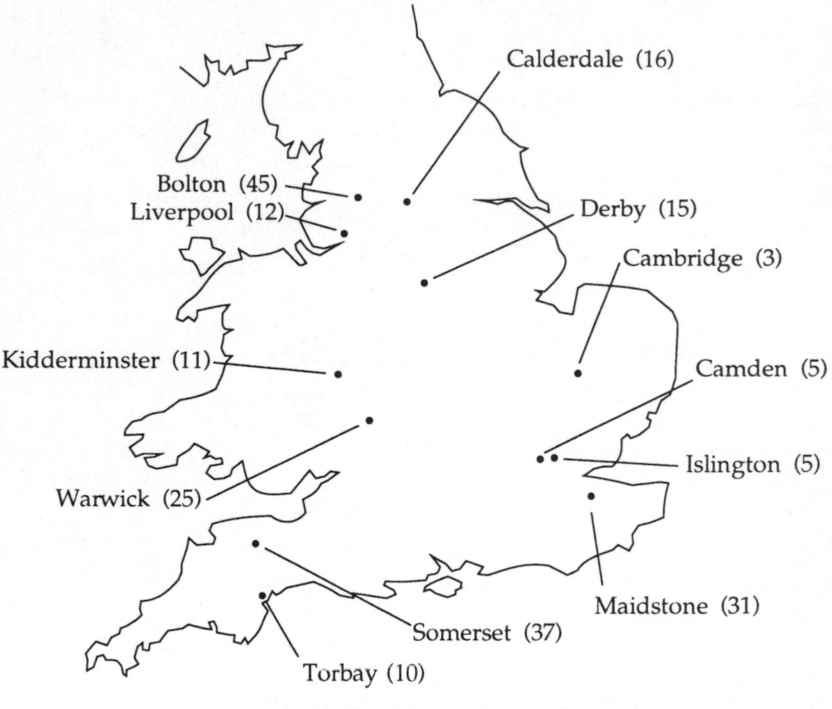

year period, and most local projects continued to help other hospital in-patients move to the community after the period of central government funding.

The projects for people with learning disabilities

The projects for people with learning disabilities varied tremendously in scale and design (see Box 2.1). Five projects intended to cater for fewer than twenty people. At the other end of the scale, one project set out to help nearly 100 people move from hospital in the first three years. In each case, hospital rundown was expected to continue after or in parallel with the pilot project. Some projects departed considerably from established models of care of the mid-1980s. For example, Maidstone introduced devolved budgets for care managers, Bolton established an innovative rural training programme, and Kidderminster was active in encouraging one of the earliest citizen advocacy schemes.

Nevertheless, as we described earlier, the pilot projects shared a number of features which were beginning to be discussed in national policy debates and which were seen to be facets of good practice in the early 1980s. One of these was that service environments for people with learning disabilities were no longer to be dominated by health care provision and principles. The philosophy of normalisation (despite its many different interpretations; Brown and Smith, 1992) and the 'ordinary life' approach (King's Fund Centre, 1982) were beginning to be widely discussed. They provided the starting point for community care planning in a number of localities. Inevitably, there were local variations on the normalisation theme, influenced by individual and collective interpretations, preferences and constraints. The 'five accomplishments' of O'Brien and Tyne (1981) provided a baseline for working with users around individually specified goals in a number of projects. Each of the projects set out to link service packages closely to needs and preferences although, for reasons we describe below, this was not always achieved.

The former hospital residents

During the three years of government funding, a range of accommodation and support services had been accessed. The people who left hospital for these new, often innovative services displayed a wide range of abilities, needs, histories, family ties and aspirations.

Half of the sample of leavers from hospital (47 per cent) were men. Half were aged between 30 and 49, 20 per cent were under 30, and the remainder were 50 or older. Many projects deliberately chose younger people. Before each person left hospital, ward staff rated their 'level of disability'. This

Box 2.1
The twelve projects

Bolton. In the three years of DHSS funding, the Bolton Neighbourhood Network Scheme helped 68 people move from five large hospitals, either to ordinary domestic accommodation rented from the local authority or a housing association, or to adult (home care) placements with families. Extensive provision for day care was made by appointing education support tutors to draw up and implement individual learning programmes, and to help people gain access to ordinary adult education services at the local college. A rural training scheme was created, offering occupational alternatives such as farmwork. At the outset, the Bolton project was jointly initiated and led by project coordinators from health and social services.

Calderdale. Twenty-five people moved from two hospitals into staffed group homes in Calderdale. Day care was provided in a resource centre, a local college of further education and an adult training centre (ATC). Parent representatives sat on the local steering group, but — as was the case virtually everywhere else — service users were not invited to participate.

Cambridge. The Cambridge project helped three young people with learning and physical disabilities leave Ida Darwin Hospital to live in an ordinary house. All three needed considerable support and care. A staff team provided and organised services on an individual basis. The project was led by the district health authority, managed by the local authority social services department, and used housing provided by a housing association.

Camden. The Camden LinC (Living in Camden) project worked with fourteen former residents of St Lawrence's Hospital in Caterham. Former hospital residents had tenancy rights in small flats or houses. This was one of the comparatively few schemes run and managed by a voluntary body — Camden Society for People with Learning Difficulties (CSMH). In the early years, the scheme had the full backing of statutory agencies, but major funding problems developed later. The project was able to tap into the housing and day care provision of CSMH, and a training project was established in the form of Applejacks Café off Camden High Street.

Derby. One of the larger projects moved people from Aston Hall and Makeney Hospitals into their own homes in the city of Derby, using a range of housing types, some arranged through housing associations. Forty-six people left the hospitals during the period of Care in the Community funding (and many more since). It was intended that these people should be able to move from one community placement to another as needs and preferences changed, and after five years a number lived independently in the community.

Islington. Five people were discharged from St Lawrence's, Leavesden, and Queen Elizabeth Hospitals into shared or single flats in two houses provided by the London Borough of Islington housing department. They were supported by residential social workers through flexible support responsive to client needs.

Kidderminster. The Disco project in Kidderminster identified a number of people in Lea and Lea Castle Hospitals who could move into houses, hostels and group homes in various parts of Hereford and Worcester. Twenty-five made the move during the period of central government funding. Comprehensive day care provision included work experience, recreational skills training and a variety of diversified day services. Existing ATCs provided day placements and work opportunities. An independent citizen advocacy scheme was encouraged, secured by separate funding.

Liverpool. One of the two projects led by Mencap supported fourteen former residents of Olive Mount Hospital in staffed group homes in Liverpool. Each group home (of four residents) was the responsibility of Liverpool Housing Trust, but managed by Mencap. Staff and care management arrangements were coordinated across the homes.

Maidstone. With the help of a project jointly managed by Kent County Council and Maidstone Health Authority, 52 people moved from Lenham and Leybourne Grange Hospitals. A range of accommodation was provided to suit different needs, and the project was one of the few to involve private sector residential care and rented housing. Devolved budgeting allowed service contracts between users and care managers. Day support was provided by social services and through special workshops.

Somerset. The project in Somerset was part of a county-wide strategy to transfer lead responsibility for service provision to the local authority. The project opened 'core and cluster' homes in Yeovil and Bridgwater to accommodate 64 former residents of Sandhill Park and Norah Fry Hospitals. A key component of the service strategy was the expectation that, after rehabilitation and training, clients would move to small group homes or other supported accommodation, with the core houses becoming resource centres.

Torbay. The Park View Society was funded to establish a hostel in Newton Abbot for ten people from Hawkmoor Hospital. The care model was based on the success of a similar facility run by the Society in Torbay. Although the project received some financial backing from the health authority, it aimed to be largely funded from social security revenue.

Warwick. A partnership between the county social services department and local Mencap societies allowed 30 people move from four local hospitals (Chelmsley, Coleshill Hall, Weston and Abbeyfield) to core and cluster or hostel facilities managed by Mencap. The project made use of local authority day support, including special education centres when appropriate.

information was available for only about half the people who moved from hospital, but it is broadly representative. Using the descriptions employed in the questionnaires at the time, staff views were as follows:

- 5 per cent of people were rated as profoundly disabled;
- 46 per cent were severely disabled;
- 30 per cent were moderately disabled; and
- 19 per cent were mildly disabled.

Although these ratings are crude and obviously subjective, they broadly indicated to local planners and developers of community care that the majority of people would need continuing and close support. This was strongly reinforced by the much more detailed descriptions of skills and behaviour gathered during assessment surveys of residents conducted in some hospitals. For example, the NDT/Wessex scales were employed in Kidderminster and Somerset. In order to get a consistent picture of hospital residents' characteristics, we interviewed hospital staff using our own standardised questionnaires. These interviews revealed a group of people with many needs for continuing support (see Box 2.2).

More than three-quarters of the group had been disabled from birth, and half had been in continuous residence in hospital for more than 21 years (one person for as long as 58 years). Not only had many of these people been resident in hospital for much of their lives, but they had maintained or developed few contacts with people in the community. Some had no regular

---

Box 2.2
Characteristics of people when in hospital

- Less than half could wash or bathe without assistance.
- Two-thirds could dress adequately without help.
- Less than one-third were literate and less than one-half numerate.
- Communication and other interactions with fellow hospital residents were rated as 'below normal' (compared to the general population) for nearly half of the sample.
- A third rarely or never participated in decisions about the roles they performed in hospital and another third only occasionally played an active part.
- Only 20 per cent could shop alone with supervision, only 13 per cent could manage their own financial affairs, and the same percentage could find their own way or use public transport.
- One half were said to be unable to organise or plan their own activities.
- Attention-seeking behaviour was a frequent or occasional problem in relation to a third of the hospital residents in the sample.
- Physical aggression or verbal abuse was reported for almost the same proportion.
- For one in ten people, it was reported that regular or occasional sexually offensive behaviour was a problem.

contact with people outside hospital. In fact, according to hospital staff, about two-thirds lacked recent, regular or close contact with the outside world, although 54 per cent were in occasional or regular contact with parents, 31 per cent with a sibling, and 14 per cent with some other relative or friend. For virtually everyone leaving hospital, it was abundantly clear that there were few possibilities for drawing upon established community contacts or family resources for significantly supplementing the formal support offered by care agencies.

During interviews with researchers, more than two-thirds of the hospital residents who later moved to the community expressed general satisfaction with where they lived (both the hospital and their own ward). They were generally satisfied with the space they had for their possessions, food, clothes and other personal belongings, how they spent their days, having enough to do, their relations with nursing and other staff, and other aspects of their lives in hospital. Despite these reasonably high levels of satisfaction with hospital, only 12 per cent wanted to continue to live there.

Hospital leavers had been selected by project staff, usually after consultation with them and with those relatives with whom they maintained regular contact. They were the hospital residents considered most suitable for the kinds of community services already available or planned. Although much of the detailed service planning *followed* the assessment of needs, some parameters were already fixed by local circumstances and agreements.

On the whole, those who moved to the community during the period of our evaluation were less likely to need close support in the community than the people who stayed: they were younger, had more social contacts with friends and family, were more likely to have had recent experience of using some community facilities, and had a greater number of 'daily living skills' and fewer behavioural problems (Knapp et al., 1992, Chap. 5). The successes of community care described in this book, including the achievement of new lifestyles and welfare improvements, are important. But we should not rush to generalise from these successes to people with *greater* needs who, under most of today's closure programmes, tend to leave hospital somewhat later. The research sample included relatively few people who might be described as 'heavily dependent', and their support in community settings may require different responses.

Although generally more independent than those who remained in hospital, the people who moved to the community nevertheless presented many challenges to themselves, to their carers, to agencies and to care staff. Almost everyone had life skills which would benefit from further development, and a number demonstrated behaviours which required well-tailored support.

3 Evaluating Community Care — Structure

The evaluation of community care was primarily concerned with the needs, outcomes and services used by individual people. Three main themes were examined:

- What does community care mean for these people with learning disabilities?
- What challenges does community care pose for agencies and carers?
- What does community care cost?

These same questions had structured our earlier evaluation of the Care in the Community programme when we had looked at outcomes, processes and costs over the comparatively short period of about one year between discharge from hospital, and interview and assessment in the community (Renshaw et al., 1988; Knapp et al., 1992).

Research findings after one year in the community

The results of the earlier short-term evaluation had been broadly encouraging. After a year in the community, most of the 356 people with learning disabilities whom we studied were doing well. They were well-supported in accommodation which was better than hospital, had acquired new skills, and they expressed satisfaction with their lives (Box 3.1).

Hospital closures generate public anxiety. Some is well-founded, particularly about the consequences for people with learning disabilities or mental health problems who are discharged into communities which are usually unfamiliar and sometimes hostile. A basic but significant achievement of the Care in the Community programme was the *successful* resettlement of a large number of long-stay hospital residents. People were not dumped in the community without care support or access to social security benefits. No one was homeless or spent time in prison or police cells during the first year in the community. Mortality and readmission rates were no higher than would be expected given the age profile of former hospital residents.

Box 3.1
Key findings after one year in the community

- People moved to well-supported and generally carefully planned accommodation.
- In most respects, community accommodation was of better quality than hospital.
- Carers did not have an unreasonable 'burden' thrust upon them.
- Users acquired many new self-care skills.
- But, in several cases, there was some exacerbation of mild behavioural problems.
- The people who left hospital were offered greater choice about their daily activities.
- They took more decisions for themselves.
- They made extensive use of ordinary community facilities, although integration remained a commonly unmet aim.
- They expressed greater satisfaction about their social networks.
- Community care was more costly than hospital. However, greater expenditure brought about better outcomes (in terms of improvements in skills and behaviour).

The centrally-funded programme provided important safeguards, contributing to these and other successes. The failings of community care are commonly due to inadequate resourcing, poor strategic management and unimaginative case-level operation. In marked contrast, most of the demonstration projects were given enhanced and protected funding from central and local sources which they used effectively, usually through rigorous care management or similar arrangements, in the context of innovative strategic planning and multiagency working.

Improvements in quality of life after leaving hospital were significant for most people, particularly in relation to life and self-care skills, and in the satisfaction the former hospital residents themselves expressed about life in community settings. However, community care was more expensive than hospital provision for more than half the sample, even after the early set-up and transition costs had been discounted. Nevertheless, when we compared the different community care arrangements, we found that higher costs tended to be associated with better quality care and a better quality of life. Smaller, more domestic community accommodation such as ordinary housing was associated with greater improvements in individual capabilities and quality of life: 'ordinary life' principles appeared to work.

We describe some of these short-term outcomes, processes and costs in more detail in later chapters.

The longer-term evaluation

The short-term effects were undoubtedly important for former hospital residents, their families and hospital and community staff. But would they last beyond the first year? Were they *honeymoon* effects associated with a high profile demonstration programme or the early excitement of the move from long-stay hospital residence? Would some of these effects disappear in the longer term or could they be maintained? Indeed, could some of the less satisfactory results after one year show improvements after five? For example, some of the vestiges of life in an institutional setting had not been thrown off after a year in the community: many people still lacked the confidence to undertake social activities or take decisions for themselves, some were denied control over their own resources, and some user-staff relations needed further improvement.

These initial difficulties were particularly encountered by those people who had spent longer in hospital prior to discharge, for they needed time to find their feet in the community — to gain familiarity and confidence, to establish contacts and make new friends, and to take control over key aspects of their lives. Also, some of the users who were able to communicate expressed dissatisfaction with life in the community. Few people had achieved much success in gaining access to the kinds of activities and social groups which are available to most members of society, and there remained new skills to acquire and new challenges to meet.

The Joseph Rowntree Foundation supported a second follow-up study which examined these twelve community care projects in the longer term. The study focused on:

- accommodation;
- quality of life;
- service utilisation;
- cost;
- service coordination via care management; and
- strategic management and joint working.

The special Care in the Community funding from the DHSS during the 1980s had been made available for only three years, and the last cheques were banked in April 1988. During the second follow-up period covered by the longer-term evaluation, all services were financed from regular or mainstream sources — local and health authority budgets, social security payments, and (though much smaller in magnitude) contributions from users and their families. The projects may have been unusual at conception and infancy — with external funding, special joint working and care management arrangements (ahead of national policy changes), high public profiles and, in some cases, high-risk innovations — but, in maturity, they were more integrated into mainstream services, although often characterised by a special identity and staff commitment.

While our evaluation started with a set of special projects unusual in their historical context, it finished in the mainstream of community care experience. As we show later, these former pilot projects have faced the same opportunities, joys, disappointments and uncertainties as most other community care services for people with learning disabilities.

Research methodology

The effects of a care system, policy or practice can be gauged by examining how far it achieves its various service quality, user welfare and resource objectives. Although our evaluation was focused on individual service users and gave them the opportunity to express their views about changes in quality of life, we do not pretend that it was emancipatory. Important elements of the research framework were necessarily inherited from our earlier evaluation because of the need to make comparisons over time. But, as far as possible, our approach was consultative and participative in an attempt to minimise the difficulties of a top-down, professionally-led research model. Our concern for user interests was reflected in the focus on the effects of community care on user welfare objectives, including collecting information directly from them and ensuring that we understood their viewpoints.

In the 'production of welfare' conceptual framework which structured our research, these are called the *intermediate and final outcomes*, although other terms could be used (Knapp, 1984; Knapp et al., 1992, Chap. 4; Cheetham et al., 1992). Intermediate outcomes include the volume and quality of services and the nature of the caring environment. Final outcomes, on the other hand, include changes in the quality of life and welfare of individual service users and those who support them. Policy-makers, planners, managers and practitioners also need evidence about the relationships between outcomes, resources and needs, and on the degree of congruence between the lives people *want* and the lives they actually lead. In attending to the equity and efficiency aims of community care — the former stressing the objective of responding consistently to similar individual needs and targeting more support where needs are greater, and the latter stressing the objective of securing better outcomes from a fixed level of spending or reducing the cost of a given level of effectiveness — we therefore required broad and detailed sets of information from the evaluation.

User outcomes is a shorthand term for differences in individual welfare over time, set against some baseline of comparison (such as individual welfare in a continuing care ward in hospital). Our primary concern was user outcomes five years after hospital discharge, and we therefore extended our longitudinal comparisons using consistent instrumentation from the hospital interviews and the initial community interviews one year after discharge. As we described earlier, most of the (former) projects adopted some variant of normalisation or an ordinary life, which acknowledges that people with disabilities are often undervalued, stigmatised and oppressed, and need support in order to create the opportunities required to lead a full and valued life as ordinary citizens (Wolfensberger, 1972; King's Fund Centre, 1982; Ward, 1985).

It was logical, therefore, that we should build our evaluation around the principle of normalisation, as captured for example by O'Brien (1986) in his 'five accomplishments' or positive life experiences. These are: *community presence* in valued community settings; *choice* or autonomy in small everyday matters and larger life-defining issues; *competence* or the ability to perform functional and meaningful activities with whatever assistance is needed; *respect* in a network of people and valued roles in community life; and community *participation*, being part of a network of personal relationships with other people. Pursuing these accomplishments is demanding for users, carers and services, and requires changes in the organisation of support and the expectations individuals hold.

We translated the 'five accomplishments' into the following research dimensions:

- skills and behavioural characteristics;
- engagement in activities (including use of services, choice and autonomy);
- morale and life satisfaction;
- social relationships and networks;
- personal presentation;
- living environments (both physical and social); and
- the organisation of care support (including care management and area-level planning).

Information was gathered during interviews which were timed to be as close as possible to four and a half years after the date of hospital discharge. (The four and a half year time elapse was chosen simply to fit in with our research timetable and to maximise the number of service users who could be interviewed within the period during which our research was funded.) For convenience we refer to them as 'five year interviews', and a few did indeed occur after five years. Other data were obtained from agency records, financial accounts, and from interviews with middle and senior managers. The format of each interview was largely determined by the instrumentation and approach in our earlier evaluation, because we saw it as important to be able to make comparisons over time. The research dimensions were translated into a set of research instruments.

The *user interview* was conducted directly with users on a confidential and one-to-one basis. We wrote directly to all users explaining the objectives and methods of the research study and seeking their informed consent, using plain English and Makaton symbols. The focus of the interview was each user's perceptions of and satisfaction with their recent life experiences, particularly those embraced by O'Brien's five accomplishments. The interview covered accommodation, social and personal relationships, privacy, engagement in activity, morale, life satisfaction, health and psychosocial functioning. Research has shown that a variety of media — such as photographs, pictures and videos — are useful for eliciting information (for example, Wagner, 1979; Conroy and Bradley, 1985; Simons et al., 1989; Booth et al., 1990) and some of these techniques (pictures and symbols) were incorporated into our user interview to facilitate participation and choice for people with limited receptive and expressive communication.

The *behaviour interview* was conducted with keyworkers or care managers. This interview covered so-called adaptive and maladaptive behaviours or, as we referred to them during the research fieldwork, *skills and accomplishments* and *behaviour*. These concepts may be defined as the effectiveness or degree with which individuals meet the standards of personal independence and social responsibility expected for age and cultural group. Adaptive behaviour refers to skills necessary for everyday functioning and independence. Our skills and behaviour interview included both positive adaptation, coping with environmental cues and demands, and maladaptive (that is, challenging) behaviours, problematic for the individual, other people or the community. There are well-established associations between challenging behaviours, client visibility, carer difficulties and the individual remaining in or returning to more restrictive accommodation, such as a hospital (Emerson et al., 1987; Borthwick-Duffy et al., 1987). We developed the instrument previously used to assess skills and behaviour to allow direct comparisons and to ensure broader coverage.

We collected information using the *personal presentation checklist* developed at the PSSRU and refined in light of experience in empirical research. Information was collected by researcher observation to reduce interrater bias. Although not the most important dimension of an evaluation of community care, personal presentation is influential for determining how others perceive and relate to us.

Physical and social aspects of the living environment exert a powerful influence on the various accomplishments and dimensions outlined above. Physical environment is important for the communication and production of cultural values (Wolfensberger, 1972) and for influencing social environment (Gunzburg and Gunzburg, 1973). The focus of the *environment checklist* was on external and internal physical features, plus the neighbourhood context and the accommodation. We also incorporated a social environment index which covered regime, social choice and opportunities, and domestic patterns and activities, with global ratings of institutionalised practices. Most of the factors which have since been identified as representing the basic rights of people living in residential support services, such as choosing when you come and go and having your own keys, are included in the index, along with evaluations of institutional control and uniformity (King et al., 1971).

Care management may be viewed as a microcosm of the service system (Wray and Wieck, 1985; Renshaw et al., 1988). It is fundamentally concerned with mechanisms for acquiring and tailoring resources to individual needs in efficient and equitable ways. Care management is a system outcome but not a client outcome. The *care management interview* thus supplemented individual and environmental assessments, and reported on relationships between needs, resources and outcomes at both macro and micro levels. We developed and used this interview schedule and made use of local care management and individual service planning documentation in order to describe this important developing facet of community care.

The *community care policy* interview was conducted with senior managers and chief officers to gain an understanding of the interpretation and translation of national and local community care policy into practice. Combined with the care management interview, it provided an overview of organisational arrangements in services and host agencies. It generated much of the material used in Chapters 8 and 9.

Three other research instruments or activities were employed, each of them described in more detail in later chapters. The *carer interview* and *staff questionnaire* gave us detailed information on the people who provided support in the community for members of the sample. Both offered respondents the opportunity to express their concerns and pleasures as well as to describe the many tasks they performed. The *client service receipt interview* (CSRI) was the means by which we collected details of the various services which people used, the services they did not use but needed, their income levels and sources, and the support they received from informal carers. The CSRI is described in more detail in Beecham and Knapp (1992) and Beecham (1994).

The comparisons within our evaluation are therefore concentrated on alternative community care settings and arrangements and, of course, the contrasting situations between hospital, early experiences in the community and longer-term consequences and opportunities for individual people. The study did not include a 'comparison group' of people with learning disabilities remaining in hospital as long-stay residents. In some respects this is unfortunate because comparisons between hospital and community care help to highlight the personal, social and economic implications of today's community care policy emphasis. However, such a comparative design is fraught with difficulties, practical as well as ethical, as services and provision are changing almost unrecognisably as hospitals run down to eventual closure, and as younger and more mobile staff and less dependent residents move away.

Construction of instruments

We do not report in detail on the individual items and measures used in the above instruments, nor on scale development and scoring. These are outlined in a little more detail in Chapter 6 when we examine the outcome domains. They are also reported in detail in Knapp et al. (1992, Chap. 5). As we have noted already, we extended the approach adopted for the DHSS-funded work to maintain comparability.

Sample size

Information was collected in interviews with 215 former hospital residents and with their support staff, paid home carers and/or care managers. For 172 of these people we had also conducted interviews in hospital; and for 203 of them we had conducted interviews in the community one year after discharge (Box 3.2). We had data on all three occasions for 162 people, and it is this group which gets most attention as we address the evaluation questions.

The study therefore concentrated on a reasonably large group of people for whom we already had detailed data from previous community and hospital interviews. The study also looked at the service systems supporting these people, and the organisational principles and operational difficulties within them. First we examine the underlying principles and practices in the next chapter, before turning to staffing, user outcomes, costs and the organisation of community care.

Box 3.2
Sample sizes

A sample of 265 people were included in the study after one year in the community. The sample fell to 203 after five years because:
- 17 people fell outside the time scale of the study (interviews after four and a half to five years);
- 14 had died;
- 23 were readmitted to hospital and were not re-interviewed;
- 3 did not wish to participate in the study;
- 2 had moved out of the area (known destination) and were not followed up;
- 3 were lost — they could not be located by the former projects.
Another 12 people were involved in the study after five years though not after one year.

---

4 Service Principles and Practices

Broad service principles

Care management, normalisation and a commitment to user involvement were the key principles adopted by the Care in the Community projects for designing and implementing support programmes for former hospital residents. Implementing the philosophy of normalisation during the first year sometimes proved difficult, particularly when badly translated, inflexibly applied, or contrary to users' preferences. Allowing users to take risks had to be weighed against public expectations and professional responsibilities, a balance that was not easily achieved. Nevertheless, by every criterion of normalisation which we examined, community accommodation after one year was better than hospital (Knapp et al., 1992, Chap. 8).

Initial conditions were favourable for services to put care principles into practice. The DHSS grant and associated conditions governing its use helped to ensure adequate funding, project influence over provider agencies, and a commitment among middle managers to link services closely to needs. When DHSS grant aid gave way to mainstream funding, it often became harder to maintain good practice. Staff support to some accommodation — particularly the houses used as staffed or unstaffed group homes — was reduced, and access to services was sometimes curtailed because of factors such as loss of individual staff, frozen posts or lack of placement opportunities. Financial streamlining and operational pruning occurred, although the joint working partnerships and collaborative arrangements established in the early years of project development were generally maintained (see Chapter 8).

However, our interest here is what was happening after five years in the community. Were broad service principles still emphasising ordinary lifestyles, choice, autonomy, opportunities for participation in activities and community integration? These are the questions addressed in this chapter.

Box 4.1
Accommodation destinations[a]

Users	Accommodation type	Definition
4	hospital	long-term in-patient
17	residential home	continuous staff cover by day, waking staff cover by night, 6 places or more
53	hostel	continuous or intermediate staff cover by day, sleeping-in or on-call, or no staff cover at night, 6 places or more
17	sheltered housing	some day staff cover, some night staff cover, scale of individual living units less than total scale of facility, clients' tenure not as residents
72	staffed group home	continuous or intermediate staff cover by day, any form of night staff cover (including none), 2-5 places
25	unstaffed group home	ad hoc or no day staff cover, on-call or no night staff cover, 2-5 places
13	foster placement	intermediate day staff (support) cover, on-call night staff (support) cover, clients moved in with established household
2	supported lodgings	ad hoc day staff cover, on-call night staff cover, clients move in with established household
9	independent living	ad hoc or no day staff cover, no night staff cover, only 1 former hospital resident accommodated. (Includes living with relatives or spouse.)
3	unclassified	

Note
a Numbers refer to the 215 people for whom we conducted interviews five years after they left hospital. They do *not* necessarily indicate typical patterns of community accommodation of former hospital residents.

Accommodation

Between them, the twelve former projects offered a wide range of different accommodation types (Box 4.1) and day support services, but a host of constraints usually meant comparatively little local variety. Rarely was there sufficient in-built flexibility to permit easy graduation between accommodation types as people's needs and preferences changed. On occasions, staff identified the need for and desire of individuals to move to other accommodation, but tight resources largely prohibited this. It was therefore rare for users to be able to exercise much choice over accommodation, and there was also relatively little correlation between accommodation type and users' characteristics (particularly skills and behaviour). Limited availability of the right kind of housing — that is, housing which was a product of the chosen service philosophy — proved to be a major constraint on community support outside residential care and nursing home settings.

This will continue to be an irritant for the foreseeable future. Services based on networks of housing and support, such as in Somerset, were able to achieve more in this regard than those in isolation, such as in Islington. However, even in the former some people had to move across service boundaries to access independent accommodation.

Whatever these accommodation achievements, most former hospital residents were still accommodated with other people with learning disabilities and in facilities with high staffing levels. A third of the sample lived in relatively large-scale staffed accommodation (hostels, residential care homes or hospitals), and a third in relatively small staffed group homes (ordinary housing). Only one in eight of the sample lived independently, and only one in four in accommodation which did not employ specialist care staff on the premises.

Although 36 per cent of the sample had moved from one type of accommodation to another since leaving hospital, few had faced the trauma of many changes, most moving only once or twice as part of an informed and shared process of individual development. Therefore, only a very small number of people had frequently changed address. The main exception was the Camden project, where resource constraints meant that some people were moved back to hsopital from what had been intended as 'homes for life' in the community. A woman in another project had moved six times within a twelve-month period. She was only temporarily happy with her living arrangements and periodically walked out, despite continued efforts to find accommodation that met her needs.

Most accommodation moves were planned and achieved, though required appropriate staff support, reflecting the changes that had occurred over the previous five years. One example was a household group which divided and moved into nearby houses. Staff support was based within one house, enabling increased independence and autonomy for one person (recognising

---

Mandy: from institution to independence

Mandy has spent most of her life living in hospital prisons and locked wards under a Home Office order. There was a lot of resistence to her move from hospital to the community, and at first she found it difficult to accept boundaries to her behaviour. However, she demonstrated her determination and ability to live in a self-contained flat with staff support. Staff worked intensively with her, especially with regard to her relations with her family and other social contacts. Recently Mandy took a second major step to independence. Five years after leaving hospital we interviewed her in her own council flat. She was happy with her life. She had chosen and bought new furniture and had her own pet cat. Her self-image was now positive and she welcomed staff from her old service for informal social visits.

---

his need for *some* support), while meeting the greater support needs of his friends.

Just over half of the people included in the study moved to more independent accommodation, largely a reflection of the service model within one project. Core and cluster and network models explicitly facilitate moves and provide developmental opportunities, although some people also moved to residential homes or hospitals within the same project. None the less, this highlights the importance of flexibility in service responses and the use of resources for meeting people's accommodation needs.

Accommodation moves were usually proactive, reflecting individual development, changing needs and abilities, and preferences. Occasionally moves were hurried and reactive, resulting from crises within the accommodation setting or the project/service itself. These precipitate moves would not have been considered under less stressed circumstances. Some moves may have generated difficulties comparable in importance to or greater than the difficulties which precipated the move in the first place. Choice under these conditions was severely constrained. For example, someone on the waiting list for local authority housing may be offered a property which does not meet their needs, but there is usually little choice about accepting. One man turned down a property because the timing was not right and later moved at a time of crisis. The house to which he eventually moved was less well suited to his needs, but was all that could be offered at the time.

Some users were able to exercise choice, but the ability to move was often dependent on the service model and its in-built accommodation opportunities, and less frequently directly related to individual circumstances or individually commissioned services. Just as the original pilot projects needed 'double funding' to start up — continued funding for hospitals at the same time as new funding for community services — so steady-state community care requires continued investment in housing in order to offer the choice and flexibility necessary for individual development.

Quality of accommodation

Accommodation was rated according to its attractiveness and degree of institutionalisation. We looked at the structure of each building, the appearance of rooms, routines and common household practices. Information came from interviews with users and staff, and from interviewer observations.

Most buildings were pleasant and non-institutional in appearance (Table 4.1), the majority having pleasant exteriors, dining rooms, living rooms and bedrooms. On the whole, they were pleasantly decorated, comfortable and reasonably located. Houses that stand out from their surroundings risk

Table 4.1
Physical environment characteristics of accommodation

	Ratings of accommodation (%)		
Physical characteristics[a]	Hospital	Community (1 year)	Community (5 years)
Exterior of building			
unpleasant	73	7	20
institutional	94	8	15
Living rooms			
unpleasant	54	3	10
institutional	83	8	13
Dining rooms			
unpleasant	73	6	15
institutional	85	10	14
Bedrooms			
unpleasant	73	5	8
institutional	82	5	7
Other rooms			
unpleasant	89	34	46
institutional	92	29	46
Appearance of food			
institutional	83	2	13
Appearance of other supplies			
institutional	87	2	13
Interior of building			
unpleasant	68	6	10
institutional	86	8	13
No. of facilities rated	135	102	113

Note
a The description 'unpleasant' includes accommodation rated as 'fairly' and 'very' unpleasant, and the description 'institutional' includes 'fairly' and 'very' institutional. Ratings were made by research interviewers during visits to accommodation settings.

creating barriers to integration in the community and, unfortunately, one house in five was distinctive in this way. Reasons varied, but in one case resulted from a school-like appearance caused by tall iron railings running along the boundary.

Few physical or social environments were considered unpleasant. Almost all were acceptable in terms of cleanliness, noise, smell and temperature (Table 4.2), although residential homes were more likely than other types of accommodation to be unacceptable. In one large house the lounge for users was shabby and yellowed. Tea-making facilities sat on a table covered in a plastic cloth, alongside a tub full of old tea bags. The owner's lounge in the next room was newly decorated and furnished.

Some independent accommodation also offered poor physical environments, perhaps because of financial constraints, for it was not every user who received support from a community care grant (or similar) to assist with the purchase of furnishings. Lack of sufficient finance had led to some people begging or borrowing from friends and support staff to help provide furniture and fittings for their homes. On the whole, however, smaller-scale accommodation came closer to achieving the standards set by normalisation than did the more congregate accommodation in which some people settled after leaving hospital.

With the aid of pictures representing different accommodation types, we asked users where they would like to live. People often chose accommodation similar to their current placement, and when they did *not*, they stated a preference for a more independent setting.

- Highly staffed group homes were the most popular choice: 31 per cent of respondents chose them, sometimes mentioning the comfort and security they derived from knowing that staff were present.

Table 4.2
Social environment characteristics of accommodation

	Ratings of accommodation (%)		
Environment characteristics	Hospital	Community (1 year)	Community (5 years)
Identifiable from surroundings	78	14	21
Poorly located	42	8	1
Acceptable temperature	93	94	99
Acceptable noise level	67	99	90
Acceptable smell	65	94	94
Acceptable cleanliness	92	94	99
Obtrusive fire precautions	42	72	76
No. of facilities rated	135	102	113

Rehospitalisation: a crisis response

Everyone in the hospital at interview was resident on a long-term basis. For Joan it was supposed to have been a temporary, emergency placement, following the breakdown of her previous community accommodation. It was obvious as a placement, because day support was provided to Joan via the ward and it was therefore familiar to her. However, it was not sufficient to meet her needs on a full-time basis, for although she had many support needs and no communication skills, Joan was more able than many people living on the ward.

Plans to move Joan to another house in the community were proving exasperating. She had been visited by a number of people who had places available in their privately-run homes — but none would take her because of her disabilities and communication difficulties. This illustrates a common difficulty of meeting the accommodation requirements of people with many support needs. For Joan her short-term emergency placement on a hospital ward appeared to have become a long-term solution. It had become home.

- Lodgings and low-staffed group homes were each the preferred options for over 20 per cent of people. Sixteen per cent chose independent living.
- A small number of people actually preferred hospital, although those who had returned to hospital did not want to remain there.
- Over 15 per cent were unhappy with the people with whom they shared their homes, and the proportion was greater for those in residential homes. More than 40 per cent of interviewees also named individuals they would prefer to live with given the choice. These included family, friends and (occasionally) support staff — although obviously these preferences were not always realistic.

Although circumstances in the community were a lot better than in hospital, it was apparent that material standards were in decline. Housing was considered to be less attractive at five years than at one year, the result of wear and tear, underfunding and higher expectations. Consequently, some accommodation was more likely to have an institutional feel, although it was rare for rooms to be considered comparable in design and standards to the levels of institutionalisation found in hospital. The external facade and the communal rooms that received the highest levels of use were more likely to be considered unpleasant and institutional after five years than after one.

Many of the staff and other carers with whom we spoke felt that accommodation was inappropriate. Commonly, this was attributed to the scale of a residence (too large or too small), overcrowding and noise. Mobility within the home was a problem for wheelchair users, who were often made more dependent upon staff than was necessary. One person, for example, spent much of his time in one place. This happened because the needs of other residents diverted attention and he was unable to get about in a manual wheelchair. In a few services, physical disabilities associated with ageing were making housing increasingly inappropriate. Without a change in the availability of accommodation, this will obviously continue to be a problem facing community care agencies as people get older and develop age-related disabilities and other needs. Siting could be a problem, with remoteness from town centres and unpleasant locations (such as proximity to a 'red light' district or living in a rundown area) being mentioned by some residents and staff. There were also difficulties with interpersonal relationships (personality clashes and incongruent lifestyles), particularly in smaller facilities. Sexuality was rarely mentioned, but had led to placement breakdown for at least one person.

Accommodation is a key requirement for successful community living, but not the only relevant factor. It makes a significant direct contribution to quality of life because of the time spent there. Housing type and characteristics may indirectly predispose to the presence or absence of other factors, such as the registration of a home, regulations and associated physical requirements (such as fire doors).

Our findings suggest fairly high levels of dissatisfaction with current accommodation, and some dissatisfaction among former hospital residents with the people with whom they share their homes.

Lifestyles in the community

Achieving an ordinary life hinges on the development of ordinary routines within the household, the use of ordinary services, and integration into the community through active participation. Was this achieved?

We found some success in supporting the development of ordinary routines. The achievements and continuing challenges of an ordinary life approach can be illustrated by examining a few key aspects of community lifestyles.

Privacy. When people live in group situations with limited space, privacy is especially important. We found privacy was respected in most houses. For example, more than 80 per cent of accommodation settings had lockable bathrooms and toilets, although in less than a third were residents able to lock their own rooms (and sometimes this had only been introduced in response to evidence of lack of respect between household members, such as theft). Most residents were able to entertain friends in their own rooms. A few stated that they were unhappy with arrangements for spending time alone. Most had single rooms, but those who shared tended to enjoy the arrangement, particularly when it was the mark of a strong friendship. Some opted to share a room if the opportunity arose. When someone moved out, staff usually avoided placing another person in the house without the informed consent of the remaining residents, and tenancy rights were respected.

Presence and participation

Three users were attending a musical at a London theatre. One person makes unusual noises when he gets excited. The group was asked to leave the theatre. The following letter highlights the conflicting rights and responsibilities experienced by people with learning disabilities and their supporters. It also illustrates the well-meaning but patronising values which can be encountered.

> I hear there was a very unfortunate incident in the theatre on Monday night when the management felt obliged to ask you to withdraw your little boy from the auditorium because of the disturbance being caused. We have many many parties of handicapped children, often as my personal guests, and very often with little treats attached. ... If you think it would be any consolation to your little boy to receive an LP or tape of the show ... I would be more than happy to send him one with my compliments.

Sexuality. Services worked with users to deal with issues in personal relationships and sexuality. These issues may have originated in hospital, or found their initial expression in community living. Although specialist services such as psychological counselling were occasionally employed to address any problems, most support came formally or informally through staff employed by the former pilot projects. This support included women's workshops, counselling in relationships, sex education such as contraception, and HIV and safer sex. Provision varied with user need and service philosophy and, unfortunately, not all services addressed such issues productively. Some people were in potentially abusive relationships, or ones which were considered inappropriate by support staff. For a few, support was negative rather than empowering and took the form of overt disapproval or 'turning a blind eye'.

Household management. Resident participation was often encouraged by involvement in household management. More than half the facilities practised joint decision-making by arranging for staff and residents to meet as a group. Others preferred decision-making on an ad hoc basis, arriving at decisions in a less formal way. Both approaches recognised the importance of participation, allowing residents more opportunities to make choices in their lives. Despite this recognition, few accommodation settings had fully autonomous resident committees.

House routine. Residents were often involved in the day-to-day running of their home. They were more likely to have all or shared responsibility for tasks within their 'personal domain' (such as making beds) than communal and household-level tasks (such as household finance). According to staff, residents largely controlled their own spending money, and almost 80 per cent were happy with the amounts of money they had available to spend.

However, broader household finance was less likely to be considered the responsibility of residents, although they took responsibility for running their households with the necessary support. Users were happy performing the various tasks and in making their contribution to the household.

Food and meals. There was usually a relaxed and flexible approach to mealtimes and over where to eat, with free use of the kitchen for snacks and drinks. Most commonly, food was bought at supermarkets and collectively prepared. Meals were considered to be good quality by most residents. Less common was the use of catering packs, bulk buying, institutional-sized equipment and rigid routines, all of which were more likely to occur in hospitals and larger community facilities. However, one place of residence did not strive to make achievements in these areas; in contrast to everywhere else, kitchen cupboards were padlocked and the kettle was of catering size. Residents were deprived of independence in an important area of their lives.

Leisure. Most people enjoyed autonomy in their use of time. They could use their rooms when they wished, and watch television or listen to the radio without restrictions. When there *were* restrictions, they were usually the product of unreasonable use of television or radio in the past, resulting in disturbance to other residents. Many people were free to make full use of community facilities (and most took advantage of this on a regular basis). Fewer than one in ten had not done so in the month prior to interview. Few people had to be home by set times at night, and two-thirds had front door keys, although the third without keys were not necessarily restricted by this — particularly where staff support was needed when going out. People often made use of local facilities such as cafés, but less commonly restaurants or pubs, and a small number attended football matches, concerts and the theatre, usually with staff support. In over half the households, residents informed staff when they went out, an arrangement that is reasonable within a shared household, and sensible for practical reasons.

Staff encouraged people to participate in social activities if it was thought that they were regularly missing opportunities, but they did not force them. This happened in three-quarters of all facilities, the aim being to ensure residents maintained some level of social life. People whose disabilities left them housebound or who needed staff support to go out, did not seem to enjoy as full a social life as others. This was certainly the case for some where support was peripatetic and limited time was allocated to tasks considered essential, regardless of whether these were priorities for the user. Staffing levels for others were too low to enable the person-to-person support necessary for participation in community activities. Those who are physically disabled or who have other additional needs are therefore likely to be most disadvantaged.

Relationships with staff. Residents were on first-name terms with staff in all but one household, and few staff wore uniforms of any description. This provides a basis from which good relationships between staff and residents can develop. Only a handful of staff were described in negative terms by residents. Most residents did not distinguish between facilities for staff and those for residents and, although one in ten facilities had separate staff toilets, not all were used. Facilities such as sleep-in rooms were accessible to residents in eight out of ten households, and few houses had separate staff offices.

The high-quality relationships sometimes reported between staff and residents were reflected in a stable working environment, staff support and time spent with residents. However, we noticed that the staff role was becoming increasingly formalised in some places. Administration was increasing, taking support worker time away from a facilitating role because of the need to record all purchases, or use spending money in ways that had not previously been necessary. The burden of accountability and record-keeping should not be transferred to staff without providing the time and space to perform additional administrative functions. This has to be a warning for managing the continued implementation of the recent community care reforms.

Ordinary life achievements

It is not easy to provide and support an ordinary life. Routines necessary for household maintenance limit resident choice and opportunities if applied inflexibly. Facilities which are busy or supported by peripatetic staff may encounter particular difficulties if tasks have to be performed at fixed times or on fixed days. Changes in staffing levels can have similar effects. If, for example, only one staff member is supporting a group of residents, there is the danger that choice, autonomy and opportunities give way to supervision, monitoring and control, characteristics ordinarily associated with institutions. The innovations of today, in care practice or care management, risk becoming the institutionalised packages of tomorrow. Careful auditing of service quality, coupled with investment in staff training, will help to prevent such developments.

Overall, as we have described in this chapter, we found that:
- ordinary lifestyles had been established within most households;
- privacy was generally respected;
- residents were involved in the day-to-day running of facilities;
- routines were usually flexible, helping to meet users' needs;
- most people exercised choices concerning a range of activities;
- staff-resident relationships were not overly formal;
- most individuals had the opportunity to manage key aspects of their lives (with staff support where necessary);
- however, institutionalisation of some accommodation and routines seemed to be creeping in, and staff were being expected to take on increasing administrative burdens.

5 Staffing

At the heart of good community care is the successful deployment of human resources, and therefore appropriate service and care management, modes of team working, rosters and training programmes. The quality of ordinary housing, as outlined previously, depends on staff qualities, attitudes and social environment in addition to the physical and material design. It is also recognised that staff abilities and availability can help determine whether people with learning disabilities enjoy well-integrated and more ordinary lives.

A variety of staffing issues emerged during our research, some developing from the context of the original pilot projects, and others from the conditions encountered in community care more widely, such as recent reforms in service management and organisation. Not surprisingly, personnel issues continued to surface as staffing difficulties were not purely a product of the process of deinstitutionalisation. This was highlighted by the finding that the issues staff raised with us concerning training, managerial support, interprofessional working, job satisfaction, and users' challenging behaviours after five years of community care echoed what had been reported four years earlier.

The most widely reported problems were low pay and poor career opportunities, particularly for those at the 'sharp end' of service delivery. It was widely believed to be largely beyond the ability of employing and managing agencies, staff themselves or their professional organisations to bring about positive change in this area. Although we witnessed staff in Somerset organising and taking action to get a better deal, the benefits were relatively marginal and short-lived. More often we witnessed the sort of dilemma facing Camden Society for People with Learning Difficulties (CSMH), where staff were employed by an organisation which was politically weak in a locally fragmented community care system. (We return to some of the issues raised by the Camden experience in Chapter 8.) The Somerset experience offers interesting lessons (see Box 5.1).

In the twelve areas covered by our study, as elsewhere in the country, community care services have been operating for some time in fluid and sometimes confused political and policy contexts. Just at the time when the former demonstration projects were joining mainstream health and social

Box 5.1
Staffing agreement in Somerset

Responsibility in Somerset for services for people with learning disabilities was transferred to the local authority. What eventually emerged was the resolution of a potentially damaging dispute between the social services department and health authority on the one hand, and NALGO and COHSE on the other. Figure 5.1 opposite illustrates the web of relationships. Among the issues that had to be resolved were the status of the mental handicap nurse and mental health officer, and the differences between NHS and local government conditions of service, particularly regarding retirement and superannuation. The social services department approached the DHSS for a transfer order for NHS staff, but received no guidance or support, being told to sort it out locally.

Outside a national framework for resolving personnel issues, themselves resulting from national policies, the outcome was a package of relatively permissive proposals tied to a joint training and retraining programme. Somerset eventually achieved one of the best examples of a personnel policy of any of the projects in the original demonstration programme. With many hospitals across the country running down to closure, and staff redeployment becoming a sensitive issue in some places, particularly where services are transferred to trusts or consortia, Somerset's experiences are certainly relevant today.

The local agreement offered:

- full recognition of nursing qualifications and experience;
- a ring-fenced policy for recruitment, designed to protect the interests of staff in post;
- half the posts in new units and vacancies awarded to NHS staff;
- appointments to managerial posts by competition;
- broadly commensurate (or better) salary scales;
- protection of accumulated benefits, such as leave and sick pay;
- local authority removal and distribution allowance (better than those under the NHS) and agreed travelling costs;
- eligibility for further training and career opportunities;
- special consideration for staff approaching retirement; and
- full entitlement to redundancy payments for NHS staff who transferred.

care provision (although a few rightly maintain they were never outside it), national policy was bringing about the most radical changes to the mainstream for 40 years. Determination to introduce local variants of national policy added to the complexity.

Staff in many former projects, including Maidstone and Islington, were faced with the authority-wide introduction of modes of working which they themselves had pioneered and refined. Many were therefore concerned that their carefully developed care management approaches or joint working arrangements would be replaced by broader systems which could damage established working patterns and partnerships.

Figure 5.1
Developing a personnel policy: the web of relationships

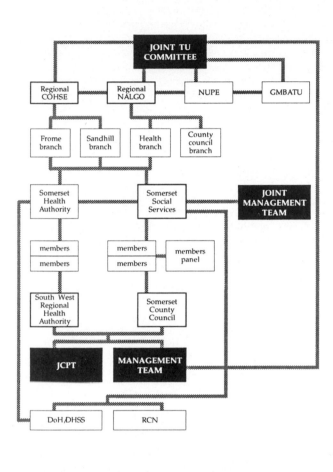

It was within this context that we examined staffing issues in each of the twelve areas. As well as talking to staff, often informally during other research fieldwork activities, we used a structured questionnaire which staff completed voluntarily and anonymously. We left a questionnaire with each of the 174 staff members with whom we had contact, including direct support staff, keyworkers, team leaders and house managers. Sixty-six people (37 per cent) completed and returned questionnaires, with response rates varying considerably from service to service. Their opinions describe the attitudes and perceptions of people working in community care in a cross-section of jobs,

Table 5.1
Job satisfaction

	Job satisfaction					
	Very satisfied %	Quite satisfied %	neither %	Quite dissatisfied %	Very dissatisfied %	Sample size N
Income	4.6	53.8	10.8	24.6	6.2	65
Job security	30.8	44.6	12.3	10.8	1.5	65
Working hours	12.3	56.9	10.8	9.2	10.8	65
Work rotas	11.1	54.0	12.7	9.5	12.7	63
Journey to work	40.6	31.3	18.8	6.3	3.1	64
Supervision	27.7	44.6	12.3	9.2	6.2	65
Peer relationships	49.2	41.5	1.5	6.2	1.5	65
Career opportunities	9.2	36.9	23.1	18.5	12.3	65
Public respect	18.5	46.2	26.2	4.6	4.6	65
Own work accomplishments	35.4	49.2	4.6	7.7	3.1	65
Skills development	18.8	60.9	12.5	3.1	4.1	64
Challenges	29.2	47.7	9.2	9.2	4.6	65
Work tasks	24.6	52.3	13.8	7.7	1.5	65
Work variety	33.8	44.6	12.3	7.7	1.5	65
Using initiative	55.4	40.0	1.5	1.3	1.5	65
General	35.4	55.4	6.2	1.5	1.5	65

services and agencies, and offer interesting perspectives on a number of relevant issues, although these are not necessarily nationally representative.

Qualifications and experience

In-house, local and national training programmes and courses in community care have not kept pace with the rapid changes in management and practice demanded by the community care reforms. There is also uncertainty about the best ways to staff the new community care system. For instance, the *Caring for People* White Paper was not prescriptive about the professional backgrounds or experiences required for care management, leaving service managers and team leaders with the task of matching experience, qualifications, attitudes and values with the requirements of the job and the employing organisation. Thus, the seemingly perennial debate about the appropriateness of nursing qualifications for community-based support work remains largely unresolved.

The picture from our survey suggests a mix of professional backgrounds and experiences in community-based work. Nine respondents had professional qualifications in social work, five in residential care and eleven in

Table 5.2
Work responsibilities

	Responsibilities			
	% Major responsibility	% Minor responsibility	% No responsibility	Sample size
Personal care	88.7	8.1	3.2	62
Health care	80.3	19.7	0.0	61
Medication	77.0	23.0	0.0	61
Administration	55.7	34.4	9.8	61
Budgeting and finance	69.4	19.4	11.3	62
Assessment	75.4	19.7	4.9	61
Advocacy	70.5	19.7	9.8	61
Service coordination	42.4	45.8	11.9	59
Community orientation	70.7	25.9	3.4	58
Teaching	70.5	18.0	11.5	61
Counselling	55.7	29.5	14.8	61
Befriending	74.2	19.4	6.5	62
Domestic	74.2	17.7	8.1	62

nursing, including one occupational therapist and one educational psychologist. A third of the respondents had previous experience of working in hospital settings, a fifth in nursing, just under half in residential care and a few in field social work. (Overall, four out of five had previous social or health care experience.) Despite funding and availability problems, three-quarters of the sample of respondents had received some form of in-service training in their present jobs.

Job satisfaction

We asked staff a number of questions relating to job satisfaction, pay, line-management support, autonomy, involvement in decision-making, career opportunities and work challenges (Table 5.1).

Although satisfaction was generally high, there were areas where relatively marked levels of dissatisfaction were reported. A third of respondents reported dissatisfaction with pay, a third with career opportunities, a fifth with rostering or shift-work, and a fifth with working hours. There was less recorded dissatisfaction in other aspects of work important for measuring performance, such as supervision arrangements, work challenges, job security and work accomplishments. Fewer than one in ten were dissatisfied with relations with colleagues, skills development or work tasks (in terms of variety or ability to take the initiative).

Areas of work and responsibilities

Self-defined work responsibilities gave an indication of the activities carried out by staff working directly with users of community services. Respondents were asked to indicate their level of responsibility (major, minor or no responsibility) for each of a range of activities (Table 5.2). Personal care was most common (89 per cent of staff assuming a major responsibility in this area), followed closely by health care (80 per cent) and administration of medication (77 per cent). These are all conventional or familiar care tasks.

Having a major responsibility for assessment, which was reported by three-quarters of respondents, suggests close ties with care management processes or at least some shared responsibility for this important core task. This is reinforced by the high proportions of staff involved in direct support work with users (86 per cent), some explicit care management responsibility (45 per cent), and a major responsibility for service coordination for individual users (45 per cent). Two-thirds of respondents held a major responsibility for budgeting and finance, illustrating that the devolved authority introduced in the demonstration programme is being maintained.

A controversial area in direct or arms-length support is the degree to which keyworkers and other service providers are able to develop a meaningful professional advocacy role. In many instances staff assume such a role because of the scarcity of alternative citizen and self-advocacy groups or befriending services, though these are not mutually exclusive. Three-quarters of staff indicated a major responsibility for befriending and for advocacy, and about half for counselling.

Decision-making

Users are now more involved in decision-making regarding ordinary day-to-day activities than previously (see Chapter 4). But at a more strategic level, for example in relation to decisions associated with care management, we found that the balance clearly rested with staff. Individual programme planning, arranging case reviews and fixing up services was predominantly the responsibility of support staff, more senior staff (usually team leaders or house managers) or jointly held. User responsibility was limited or non-existent.

Thus, the community services which had achieved laudable devolution of responsibility for, among other things, assessment and purchasing, had generally not succeeded in including users in decision-making, particularly on issues where involvement was potentially complex or time-consuming.

An emphasis on shared and democratic styles of decision-making among *staff* was maintained by most of the twelve services. This was to be expected of a philosophy of care where staff had a stake in quality support and a sense

---

Home care

When Christine left hospital she moved into a flat where she lived alone, with staff support. This arrangement broke down fairly rapidly and she moved temporarily into the home of Pat, an adult placement carer, an arrangement which eventually became permanent. Pat described her as being at risk during her stay at the flat, for despite appearing to be extremely capable she is in need of a lot of direct and indirect support.

Christine has little understanding of money management and, as someone who is very sociable, felt lonely in her flat. Making friends was hard, and those she did make were much younger than her and were sometimes willing to take advantage of her. On one occasion money was stolen from her fuel meter. Staff found they could not provide the necessary support to help Christine overcome these sorts of difficulties. Adult placement was seen as an appropriate short-term arrangement. She made a couple of short visits to Pat's house. She decided to stay and has been sharing her home ever since.

Over the years Christine has become part of the family, although there are sometimes quite severe stresses associated with the arrangement. She is now good friends with one of Pat's daughters, who lives nearby.

This arrangement gives Christine her freedom, although she occasionally abuses it, while enabling support which prevents the recreation of circumstances which led to her moving from her flat. It *has* been a positive move, one that has provided a sense of stability, value and worth for Christine who now very much feels part of a family and the wider community.

---

of belonging, and was symptomatic of a degree of autonomy from central management. Shared decision-making by staff was frequently seen in peer review and the search for consensus. Half of the staff respondents reported that they met with colleagues as an organised group at least weekly, 40 per cent at least monthly, and 6 per cent daily (presumably in more informal circumstances, such as hand-overs).

Home carers

About half of all English local authorities currently operate home care schemes which support adults, although only around 2,000 places were available nationally in 1990 (Dagnan et al., 1990). A small number of people in our sample were supported in home care placements – living with families (not their own) – and we examined the needs and experiences of their carers.

Interviews were conducted with seven home carers in two areas. All were women. None was related to the users, although some had known them prior to placement through informal contact or voluntary work with hospital or community services, and through previous paid employment. Some but not all were paid.

Home carers sometimes found difficulty in coping with their support responsibilities. This included the changing relationships and family dynamics sometimes triggered by the caring role and the new member of the household. As might be expected, challenging behaviours, attention-seeking or stereotyped behaviour, or simple mood changes all took their toll. Training and occasional additional support are important for helping carers to continue to provide good quality care. We found that training ranged from little or nothing to targeted workshops and courses (introductory and further training). A number of carers had not received training for some time, raising the question of whether their training needs were fully met.

Levels of support provided by home care varied enormously, with one user receiving no support with self-care, and another requiring and receiving help with almost everything. Some carers obtained direct or indirect support from other family members, particularly but not exclusively those living in the same household. It was sometimes difficult to arrange breaks from caring and, when respite was available, it could be expensive. Financial support was considered inadequate by some, with financial uncertainties contributing to carer stress. The relationships that developed were described by some as having beneficial effects on families by encouraging the development of better understanding, attitudes and tolerance.

Overall, it appeared that carers needed:

- regular contact and support from services;
- regular and flexible respite with access to emergency support;
- training prior to and during caring; and
- adequate financial resources without penalties or disincentives.

Staff development

None of the staffing issues described in this section is likely to be easily resolved, particularly in a period of changing management, provision and funding. However, the former projects in our study demonstrated that agencies are better armed to respond to the challenges and changes demanded by community care with supportive and innovative management, tailored personnel policies, clear guidelines for practice and operational policies.

The growth of contracting and service commissioning in each of the areas demanded roles and skills that services did not always have on tap. Most services, with the exception of those led or supported by large public service agencies, found the necessary expertise and competence difficult to develop or secure, particularly at public sector rates of pay. Similarly, staff in places like Camden and Maidstone were often shifted around as services and structures were reorganised, sometimes eroding morale and job satisfaction. Our respondents argued that the policy guidance from central government has provided little help for public or voluntary organisations wanting to define new roles and to target training and salaries appropriately. A classic example is in relation to care management. Yet there is no doubt that the future success of community care will hinge as much on the commitment, competence and attitude of the people who work in middle management and front-line jobs as on new policies, structures and procedures. Desirable community care hinges on valuing users and staff. We have noticed how practice in some services is becoming more institutionalised. Until the efforts and work of staff are recognised and rewarded, community care risks falling short of its potential.

6 Outcomes and Effectiveness

Support and integration

Common concerns about community care emphasise the dangers of neglect, victimisation, and social and economic marginalisation of people with disabilities. However, five years after leaving hospital, the people whose lives and opinions we examined in this study were well supported in the community.

Among the findings from our monitoring of quality of life, we found:

- People were not left to fend for themselves; all were in planned accommodation and most had care management or keyworker support.
- Most were living in staffed, specialist accommodation, and those who were not tended to be the less disabled and the more independent, possessing better self-care skills and other abilities.
- Lack of employment remained a major problem for everyone. Associated with it was the problem of low income (exacerbated by the perverse incentives within the benefit system) which restricted choice and limited opportunities for participation in everyday activities.
- Mortality rates were no higher than for a group of people of similar age and with their disability. No one had committed suicide.
- No one had been charged with an offence or had been imprisoned, although there *was* evidence of some minor chargeable offences, and a small number of people had come into contact with the police.
- There was no evidence of neglect and little of community victimisation. Where the latter occurred, services intervened as advocates for users and, if possible, as educators for the community.

In these respects, the situation five years after hospital discharge parallels what was found earlier (Knapp et al., 1992, Chaps 12 and 13). At the very least, services had avoided the worst 'failings' sometimes raised by the media in stories about care in the community and reported from other countries.

But what of the more 'positive' aspects of quality of life: those dimensions which are important not only for people with disabilities but which are valued by all of us? How well, for example, did care in the community measure up to the 'five accomplishments' (see Chapter 3)? We examined the effects of community care on the welfare and quality of individual lives, and changes therein (the so-called *user outcomes*), by focusing on a number of individual skills and accomplishments, the more common behavioural problems sometimes associated with learning disabilities, morale and life satisfaction, social contacts and social networks, employment and income, and personal presentation. We were interested in each of these dimensions after five years in the community, and changes since the previous evaluation after one year in the community. Choice and autonomy, which are also relevant to outcome dimensions, were described in Chapter 4.

Skills and accomplishments

Hospital wards offer few opportunities for residents to participate in everyday activities or to perform 'ordinary' daily tasks. Shopping for groceries or clothes, for example, is usually out of the question, and — in the normal course of events — few residents have the chance to help with food preparation, cooking or laundry. Few handle money and many people have lost or never acquired numeracy and literacy skills. For many people, outings from the hospital to visit friends or relatives are rare events.

If people with learning disabilities are to succeed in the community — to attain a greater degree of independence and participate in ordinary, everyday

---

A move to more independent living

Jack had left hospital to move into a fairly large voluntary agency hostel, which by the end of five years included a couple of respite beds. The hostel provided places for people with a whole mix of abilities. Jack was one of the most able, and had later moved to a group home. For a number of reasons, this move didn't work out and Jack chose to move back to the hostel.

By the time we visited him again, five years after he had left hospital, Jack had moved into his own council flat. He had regular but limited support from a support worker he considered more of a friend than a member of staff. When we visited Jack he was still settling into the flat which both he and staff from the hostel had worked hard to furnish. He felt a great deal of pride in at last having his own home.

Despite this achievement, Jack was still very dependent on the hostel for both psychological and practical support. Although it was hoped this would lessen with time, the hostel, not surprisingly, was central to his life. Most of his friends — other residents and support staff — were still there and his frequent visits were often social. Jack had few friends apart from these and other people who formed part of the local voluntary agency network. It therefore seems that without a social network outside the agency, Jack — despite his many skills — will continue to depend on the agency for a long time to come.

activities alongside people without disabilities, perhaps to get a job or take a training course — then key social skills must be learned. Different opportunities for demonstrating and improving abilities present themselves to people. We hypothesised that improvements would be observed because of the attention paid to these skills.

Our research therefore included the examination of skills attainments in hospital and in the community. We interviewed staff who knew users well, asking them about 29 different 'skills', including life-care, self-care and social skills. The schedules to measure skills and behaviour were developed from the Social Behaviour Scale (Wykes, 1982) and the Disability Assessment Schedule (Holmes et al., 1982). Details of scale development are given in Knapp et al. (1992, p.90 et seq). Table 6.1 gives the percentages of the sample demonstrating either improvement or deterioration between successive interviews in relation to each of these skills (that is, between hospital and one year after discharge, and between one and five years after discharge). A small number of changes were statistically significant.

After one year in the community, former hospital residents had acquired many new skills. Four years later there were further improvements in skills acquisitions, although in only four areas:
• managing their own financial affairs;
• taking up opportunities to use community facilities;
• independently planning or organising weekly activities; and
• counting and handling money.

Across the whole sample, some skills appeared to deteriorate (such as writing, and appearance if left to own devices), but changes were not significant.

In the first year after leaving hospital, most people participating in our survey had acquired numerous basic self-care skills which they had never previously had an opportunity to learn or which had been dormant during their years in hospital. These included dressing, cooking, basic housework, shopping, conversation, and finding one's way around. Some of these abilities were learned or re-learned in hospital-based rehabilitation programmes. In the subsequent four years in the community, achievement of skills emphasised those which develop through practice, experience and familiarity, and which are perhaps dependent on building up confidence. However, the few improvements in the later period were in areas central to the continued development and maintenance of independence.

Overall, when individual items are summed into a total skills 'score' (a crude but indicative summary), we find significant improvements in the first year after leaving hospital, but not thereafter (Table 6.2). Indeed, an examination of correlation coefficients suggests that people who did better in the first year may have fared worse in the next four years. If we look at these trends more closely, we find that there is some convergence over time — people with low skills levels in hospital improving markedly in the short

Table 6.1
Skills changes between hospital and community

Item description[b]	Hospital to community (T1→T2)[a]				Community to community (T2→T3)[a]			
	Worse[b] %	Better[b] %	Significant changes p	+/-	Worse[b] %	Better[b] %	Significant changes p	+/-
Vision	25	7	.001		16	15		
Hearing	7	9			9	6		
Mobility	18	12			16	9		
Conversation, social mixing with other clients	19	47	.001	+	35	25		
Initiation of conversation/interaction with other clients	27	51	.002	+	27	31		
Non-verbal communication	30	38			36	30		
Length of conversations	16	23			17	21		
Clarity of speech	20	25			21	21		
Eating habits at mealtime	37	30			27	40		
Does fair share of collective tasks	17	38	.016	+	36	26		
Task-sharing with other clients	28	28			33	34		
Argues with other clients	39	45			49	40		
Participation in decisions re. roles	15	63	.000	+	22	40		
Washing and bathing self	25	36	.013	+	33	34		
Dressing	20	41	.000	+	23	25		
Cooking and getting meals alone	13	55	.000	+	30	20		
Basic housework and care of clothes	23	51	.009	+	39	36		
Shopping alone	22	58			32	29		
Manages own financial affairs	25	25			17	43	.002	+
Finds way around	11	22	.000	+	29	39		

Item	%	%	p	+/−	%	%	p	+/−
Uses amenities in community (church, pub, ...)	5	83	.000	+	16	10		
Has missed opportunities in last month to use these facilities	43	19	.008	−	25	82	.000	+
Independently plans/organises weekly activities	26	38			23	43	.017	+
Understanding communication	13	23			14	16		
Reading	11	18			21	16		
Writing	10	26	.031	+	22	10		
Counting and handling money	19	31			14	36		
Looking after own clothes and possessions	32	43			35	41	.008	+
Appearance if left to own devices	32	50	.019	+	48	32		

Notes

a   Sample size is 162 people for whom we have data at all three assessment points. Missing observations on a few clients on a few items reduce sample size for some individual tests.

b   Percentage remaining the same is 100 — percentages getting worse or better. All items except 'Has missed opportunities ...' have three categories of response; the exception had two (Yes/No).

c   Using the Wilcoxon test to examine significance of changes between two assessments. p indicates significance level; +/− indicates whether the significant change was for the better (improvement over time) or worse (deterioration over time).

Table 6.2
Summary skills and behaviour scores and differences

	Mean	Standard deviation	Sample	Significance
Skills score				
hospital	60.7	11.0	162	
community after 1 year	64.5	9.6	162	
community after 5 years	64.6	10.3	162	
Skills changes				
between hospital and 1 year	3.8	7.3	162	.000
between 1 year and 5 years	0.1	7.0	162	.771
between hospital and 5 years	3.9	8.5	162	.000
Behaviour score				
hospital	68.2	4.0	161	
community after 1 year	67.1	5.4	161	
community after 5 years	66.5	5.8	162	
Behaviour changes				
between hospital and 1 year	-1.1	6.4	161	.067
between 1 year and 5 years	-0.6	6.3	161	.305
between hospital and 5 years	-1.7	6.5	162	.002

term but then stabilising, and those who left hospital with more skills changing very little thereafter (Figure 6.1). The simple correlation between the two differences in skills levels, that is, between the difference after a year in the community and the difference after the next four years was -0.30 (significant at $p<0.01$).

Why did this occur? Certainly in the first year after leaving hospital, changes in the welfare of individuals were heavily influenced by differences in the care arrangements and practices adopted by different pilot projects. In the longer term, with the end of special programme funding and the transformation of most services from pilot projects to mainstream provision, community care practices showed less variation across the sample of areas. (This undoubtedly led to the suppression of 'excellence' in some cases, but also followed from the diffusion of good practice.) However, our observations from fieldwork and discussions with staff suggest that only part of the convergence of user welfare can be explained by this standardisation of service responses. Expenditure constraints or reductions have made it harder to justify the continued pursuit of complete independence and competence for a few people when the majority are still in need of help to acquire more fundamental skills. There is, moreover, a possible ceiling to improvements in some skills, particularly where individuals have already achieved a high level of competence.

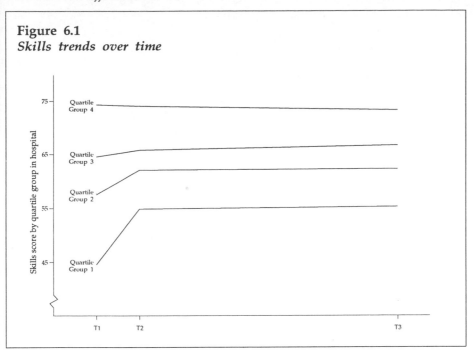

Figure 6.1
Skills trends over time

Older people within the sample were among those who were most skilled at the time of the hospital evaluations, but there was no apparent age-related deterioration in the community. We examine these and other interpersonal differences later in the chapter.

Behaviour changes

Challenging or unusual aspects of behaviour such as aggression, screaming or self-stimulation can make an individual conspicuous in the community, perhaps leading to lack of respect by others, neglect or even victimisation. Some aspects of personal behaviour — such as incontinence at night, suicidal preoccupations, wandering or damage to property — can also impose high, perhaps disproportionate, demands on services and other users. Improvements or developments in behaviour can be aided by, and can themselves foster, integration, independence, self-determination and choice.

In our interviews we asked staff about key aspects of behaviour. Our questions covered 26 quite diverse dimensions, including depression, aggression, obsessional behaviour, incontinence and attention-seeking. The full list of items is given in Table 6.3, which reports the percentages of people whose behaviour either improved or deteriorated between successive assessments.

Table 6.3
Behaviour changes between hospital and community

Item description[b]	Hospital to community (T1→T2)[a]				Community to community (T2→T3)[a]			
	Worse[b] %	Better[b] %	Significant changes p	+/-	Worse[b] %	Better[b] %	Significant changes p	+/-
Depression or weeping	26	29			19	24		
Suicidal preoccupations	7	2			1	6		
Anxiety, panic, phobias	31	20			28	31		
Slowness of movement	27	28			30	26		
Underactivity	32	30			31	40		
Overactivity	23	19			29	21		
Elated or euphoric behaviour	25	21			16	22		
Odd gestures, mannerisms	54	31	.030	−	39	46		
Acting out delusions, hallucinations	9	7			15	9		
Attention-seeking behaviour	46	24	.030	−	24	35		
Aggressive or violent behaviour	32	35			39	25		
Obsessional behaviour	25	17			31	19		
Self-injury	12	7			13	12		
Stealing (e.g. food, cigarettes)	19	20			13	17		
Collecting, hoarding meaningless items	22	22			34	24		
Shouting, swearing, offensive, screaming	44	34			36	32		
Incontinence during the day	17	16			17	14		
Incontinence at night	21	14			12	20		
Confused	40	24			36	33		
Objectionable at night	24	12			24	20		
Awake at night	40	16	.003	−	37	28		

Accuses others of doing harm, stealing	28	23	27	28	–
Wanders or runs away (if not supervised)	6	10	16	6	.034
Stereotyped repetitive activities, echolalia	35	25	42	31	.041
Sexually offensive behaviour	8	11	10	8	–
Any other problems	24	37	26	22	–

Notes

a   Sample size is 162 people for whom we have data at all three assessment points. Missing observations on a few clients on a few items reduce sample size for some individual tests.

b   Percentage remaining the same is 100 — percentages getting worse or better. All items except 'Has missed opportunities ...' have three categories of response; the exception had two (Yes/No).

c   Using the Wilcoxon test to examine significance of changes between two assessments. p indicates significance level; +/– indicates whether the significant change was for the better (improvement over time) or worse (deterioration over time).

After the *first year* in the community, summing the various behaviour indicators into an overall 'score', the sample of people with learning disabilities showed no deterioration in behaviour compared to the situation in hospital (Table 6.2), although in three component items, there were significant deteriorations:

- odd gestures and mannerisms;
- attention-seeking behaviour; and
- sleeplessness at night (Table 6.3).

These early deteriorations had disappointed care staff, and may have been due to greater visibility in the community or the greater demand or stress encountered in settings outside hospital as community care staff helped former hospital residents improve their life and self-care skills and undertake more activities away from home. On reflection, it is perhaps not surprising that there were some short-term deleterious consequences from such a major change of lifestyle.

In the longer term — over the subsequent four years of community residence — there were few further behavioural changes. In *aggregate* — summing the 26 items listed in Table 6.3 into an overall 'behaviour score' — there were no such changes, and the only individual items to show significant changes were:

- the tendency to wander or run away; and
- stereotyped, repetitive activities (Tables 6.2 and 6.3).

In both cases, more people showed more deteriorations than improvements. The apparent behavioural decline could be a function of social environment and staff attribution, but could also be a result of the difficulty in securing specialist interventions when people exhibit challenging behaviours. One of the behavioural problems — the tendency to wander or run away — might also be a simple consequence of growing confidence and familiarity with surroundings. In two other areas — aggressive or violent behaviour, and falsely accusing others of doing harm or stealing — there appeared to be deteriorations, but neither of the changes was statistically significant. Although over the full five-year period since hospital discharge there was an overall deterioration in behaviour, this was still relatively small and apparently confined to areas which are less central to the success of integration and for the achievement of an ordinary life in the community.

People who did relatively well in their first year in the community were comparative *under*-achievers in the next four years. The simple correlation between changes over the first year and changes over the next four was -0.47 (significant at p<0.01). If we look at different groups of people distinguished by their behavioural characteristics in hospital (Figure 6.2: note that these are *not* the same groupings as in Figure 6.1), we see that the increase in mildly challenging behaviours appears to be a longer-term phenomenon, and may be due to the greater demands or stresses encountered in community settings. Changes in medication levels may have played a part. There are also issues

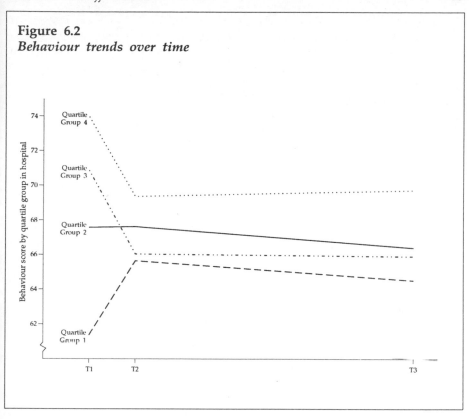

Figure 6.2
Behaviour trends over time

related to norms and expectations of people: what is readily tolerated in hospital may be more obtrusive and less readily tolerated in more public settings.

It is perhaps not surprising that skills and behaviour levels are closely related: people who demonstrate competence in one area tend to demonstrate competence in the other, with *changes* in skills and behaviour also linked. The simple correlation between aggregate skills and behaviour scores after five years was 0.47 (significant at p<0.01). People who improved between hospital and the first community assessment on one dimension were also likely to improve on the other (correlation of 0.37; p<0.01), and there was a similarly close link between improvements on skills and behaviour in the later four years in the community (correlation of 0.45; p<0.01).

Skills and behaviour differences

Thus far we have examined users as a group, but there were marked individual differences in the experience of living in the community and its

Table 6.4
Skills and behaviour by type of accommodation

	Aggregate score and sample size after 5 years			
Accommodation 5 years	Skills		Behaviour	
after leaving hospital	Score	N	Score	N
Hospital	49.0	4	62.1	4
Residential care home	55.3	17	65.3	17
Hostel	64.8	53	66.1	53
Sheltered housing	69.0	17	70.4	17
Staffed group home	63.0	72	66.1	72
Unstaffed group home	72.8	24	70.6	24
Adult placement	57.1	13	62.7	13
Supported lodgings	79.5	2	62.7	13
Independent living	73.8	9	67.8	2
Unclassified	76.0	3	71.7	3
Total[a]	64.6	214	66.8	214

Note:
a Skills and behaviour scores *for the full sample* after five years in the community. Overall, this group of 214 people does *not* display different skills or behaviour from the group of 162 for whom we have data over all three research periods (see Table 6.2).

impact. Table 6.4 shows users' skills and behavioural characteristics in relation to their place of accommodation. The differences between accommodation types are statistically significant ($p<0.001$). Those people in supported lodgings, homes of their own ('independent living') and unstaffed groups homes have higher skills levels than others, but there is a less straightforward association between intensity of staffing at the place of accommodation and behaviour.

Other patterns of variation in the skills and behaviour characteristics of people after five years in the community were also found. For example, there was a strong link between these characteristics and age, the older people being more skilled (mean score of 69.0 for those aged 60 or older, 65.6 if aged 45-59, 62.8 if aged 30-44, and 56.4 if aged under 30; $p=0.002$), and had fewer behavioural problems (mean scores of 69.3, 67.7, 65.1, 65.0; $p=0.033$). There was not, however, a significant difference between men and women in aggregate skills or behaviour.

Because of the many potential associations with skills and behaviour, some of which may actually be disguising more fundamental (but not directly observed) links, we used multivariate statistical analyses to tease out the relationships. We were interested in exploring which, if any, individual, accommodation, organisational and resource factors were associated with

Table 6.5

'Explaining' variations in skills and behaviour in the community, five years after leaving hospital

Explanatory variables[a]	Skills		Behaviour	
	β	Sig.	β	Sig.
Constant term	22.63	.000	41.75	.000
In-patient hospital care — used	5.77	.004	–	–
Community nurse (CMHN or other) — used	-3.50	.024	-2.63	.038
Social club — used	2.64	.021	–	–
Medical consultant (community) — used	-4.67	.003	-4.57	.000
Speech therapist — used	-6.34	.000	-2.90	.006
Physiotherapist — used	–	–	2.56	.081
Transport — used	–	–	2.47	.029
Residents can keep pets	2.38	.050	2.55	.007
Residents have own front door keys	7.99	.000	2.88	.006
Users cook their own meals	–	–	2.90	.019
Dining rooms rated as domestic; not institutional	2.36	.060	2.46	.063
Dining rooms rated as pleasant, attractive	–	–	-3.08	.021
Bedrooms rated as poor quality	-3.59	.016	–	–
Bedrooms rated as reasonable	–	–	2.19	.068
Accommodation easily identified within surroundings	7.42	.000	4.53	.002
Accommodation near undesirable sites	-7.49	.000	–	–
Care management by residential social worker	–	–	-5.44	.000
Skills score after one year in the community	0.59	.000		
Behaviour score after one year in the community	–	–	0.30	.001
Sample size	110		110	
R^2 and $\bar{R}^2$	0.73	0.70	0.59	0.53
F and significance	22.40	.000	9.64	.000

Notes

a All explanatory variables except skills and behaviour scores are 'dummy variables', taking the value 1 if an individual has the listed characteristic and the value 0 otherwise.

– indicates that variable was not included in the equation as it did not reach statistical significance.

differences in the aggregate skills and behaviour scores after five years of community residence. Was there, for example, a link between the use of certain community or hospital services and individuals' skills or behaviour levels? Were community accommodation characteristics associated with skills and behaviour? How much continuity was there over time; that is, to what extent were levels of skills and behaviour after five years in the community a reflection of their earlier levels? These were the kinds of question which underpinned our analyses. We took the aggregate skills score after five years for each individual as the independent variable (to be 'explained'), and the measures or indicators of service use, accommodation features, individual characteristics and so on as the independent (or 'explanatory') variables in a series of multiple regression analyses. We then did the same with aggregate behaviour score as the dependent variable. The estimated equations pick up a mixed collection of associations, some of which are not necessarily causal.

The summary results of our multiple regression analyses are given in Table 6.5, where we report the final and 'best' equation for each of the two dependent variables. By 'best' we mean that each equation is the more parsimonious representation of the associations between skills (or behaviour) and the various explanatory factors, with each of the latter being statistically significant as a predictor (that is, the association that is unlikely to have occurred by chance).

We should first note that the equations predict or 'explain' 73 per cent of the observed variation in skills score after five years in the community, and 59 per cent of the variation in behaviour score. However, a large part of each of these 'explanatory powers' is attributable to individuals' skills and behaviour characteristics four years earlier (when the previous rounds of interviews and assessments were carried out). In other words, there is a strong thread of continuity over time in both skills and behaviour attributes. This is, of course, exactly what we reported earlier in the chapter (see, for example, Table 6.2). This continuity over time is one of the reasons why it is difficult to interpret some of the revealed relationships in the estimated equations, but it is an essential factor in the equations because it standardises for the attributes of people at an earlier date. Nevertheless, a number of other characteristics are significantly associated with interpersonal differences in abilities.

The associations summarised by the equations in Table 6.5 have two broad interpretations. Some associations probably reflect the influences of user needs on service utilisation and accommodation type, for the stability of skills and behaviour over time make it difficult to disentangle the causal connections. In other words, an individual's characteristics (and needs) after a year in the community influenced the kinds and amounts of services which they were offered, but their characteristics altered relatively little over the next four years. The result was a strong correlation between service use and characteristics after five years in the community. Some other associations reflect the influences of service utilisation on user skills and behaviour. We can see these twin interpretations clearly in relation to the service utilisation variables themselves, for in-patient hospital admissions, social club attendance, physiotherapy and transport support all have positive associations with skills and/or behaviour in the community (potential 'production' or improvement effects), while community nurse support, consultations with medical practitioners (in the community) and speech therapy have negative associations (potentially interpretable as needs effects). Our examination of costs in the next chapter will shed further illumination on the links between individual characteristics and service utilisation, though within a less ambiguous causal framework.

Among the other factors significantly associated with skills and behaviour scores after five years in the community are some features of the social environments of accommodation, including having one's own front door key, the degree of 'domesticity', the quality of the bedrooms, and location. Some of the linkages are complex and reflect a web of interconnections between individual circumstances, accommodation characteristics and support environments.

The micro- and macro-organisational features of care in the community are described in more detail in Chapters 8 and 9. Only one feature appeared to be associated with skills and behaviour: care management by residential social workers was associated with lower behaviour scores. This is a pure 'needs effect', for it was those people with greater behavioural problems who were more likely to be accommodated in settings with resident staff (Table 6.4).

We did not have data on all of the factors which could be hypothesised to be associated with variations in users' skills and behaviour characteristics (and the effective sample size is too small to conduct equivalent analyses for morale and life satisfaction, social contacts or other aspects of quality of life discussed below).

After adjusting for all of the factors included in the two equations in Table 6.5, we found *no* differences in skills or behaviour scores after five years between accommodation types or sectors.

As we reported earlier, changes in skills and behaviour scores between the one-year and five-year interviews were not significant overall, but some individuals experienced quite marked improvements or deteriorations. We could find very few personal or environmental characteristics associated with these changes, except for skills and behaviour four years earlier. Higher support package costs were *not* associated with greater or smaller changes in skills or behaviour.

Table 6.6
Summary morale and life satisfaction scores[a]

	Mean	Standard deviation	Sample	Significance
Cantril's Ladder (global morale)				
hospital	3.8	1.3	100	
community after 1 year	4.9	1.7	95	
community after 5 years	5.9	1.6	141	
Cantril's Ladder changes				
between hospital and 5 years	1.5	2.6	71	0.00
between hospital and 1 year	1.2	3.0	50	0.01
Psychosocial Functioning Inventory (PFI)				
hospital	38.7	6.4	120	
community after 1 year	40.9	6.1	135	
community after 5 years	40.2	6.7	114	
PFI changes				
between hospital and 5 years	2.1	8.5	77	0.06
between hospital and 1 year	3.1	6.9	75	0.00
Depression Inventory				
hospital	11.4	7.9	97	
community after 1 year	9.6	7.0	123	
community after 5 years	10.1	7.2	102	
Depression Inventory changes				
between hospital and 5 years	-2.4	9.6	58	0.08
between hospital and 1 year	-2.9	8.9	56	0.03

Note

a None of the changes between the one-year and five-year interviews was significant.

Morale and life satisfaction

Whenever possible we asked service users about their quality of life. Earlier we reported their views about the nature and quality of accommodation. Another important part of our interview with them addressed their more general feelings, likes and dislikes, worries and aspirations. Interviews were conducted in hospital and after one and five years in the community.

We used three summary scales developed by other researchers. Cantril's Ladder is a simple global indicator of life satisfaction, and was used in parallel with pictorial forms ('happy, neutral and sad faces') for the present study, making it easier to comprehend and administer (Cantril, 1965). The morale subscale of the Psychosocial Functioning Inventory (PFI) was used to ask users how often in the past month they felt emotions such as fear, boredom and anger (Feragne et al., 1983). The third instrument was the Depression Inventory of Snaith et al. (1971), which is used to detect fairly short periods

---

A person from a minority community

Ashuk had been renamed Brian by staff working at the hospital he lived in. It was thought it may originally have occurred because staff felt unable, or were unwilling, to pronounce his name. The name Brian had remained with him over the years. Few now called him Ashuk and people were sometimes unaware of his Asian name.

Ashuk lived in a large housing association-owned house with one other man. Both had high levels of disability and associated support needs. Both also had challenging behaviours.

Ashuk and his co-resident had lived in the house since leaving hospital, originally with more people. As the house was really too big for the two of them — it was probably big enough for six — there were plans for them to move into a smaller dwelling.

Recently, the importance of Ashuk's Asian identity had been recognised, along with the need to foster and develop it. Consequently, contact was being made with his own community through social events, although the experience was not proving entirely successful. There had been success in linking him with an Asian keyworker, and in the recruitment of an Asian volunteer. Despite these efforts, barriers to integration were being created via 'service rationalisation'. Support levels had been halved, leaving only one person working at any one time. The potential outcome of this is an environment where social lives may be constrained, and social opportunities are more limited for both residents. In particular, they may deny Ashuk access to his own identity.

---

of depressive illness or prolonged periods of sadness. Sample sizes are smaller for these indicators of users' own views than with other instruments because not everyone was able or wanted to participate in our interviews (although our visual aids helped people with little or no verbal communication or signing skills). Those people who did take part in our interviews reported greater satisfaction with their lives in the community than in hospital. There were no changes in morale and life satisfaction between the two community interviews, although statistically significant improvements had been recorded during the first year in the community (Table 6.6).

Social contacts and relationships

Social contacts and relationships contribute significantly to quality of life. We gathered information on both the composition of, and users' satisfaction with, their social circles. (Leisure activities are described in Chapter 7.) People had three levels of contact with other people: with co-residents and friends, friends who lived elsewhere (including friends outside services), and family.

Most sample members who were able and willing to participate in the interview reported having a number of friends, although generally few in

> ### Rachel: using technology
>
> When Rachel first moved out of hospital she pulled herself around the house on the floor. Her verbalisation, facial expressions and signing were not readily understood and were reflected in her challenging behaviours, mainly biting her hands and lips and screaming. Her communication difficulties clearly caused considerable frustration. She was unable to engage in everyday decision-making. Her new communication card system worked well, but soon proved inadequate for her expressive development as she gained more control over her surroundings, made choices and let her preferences be known. A new speech pack with interchangeable overlays soon took over as the main medium of communication. With her motorised chair and speech pack, Rachel is now quite independent, and is able to go to the jazz club or pub when she wishes. She can initiate or join in conversations and is generally better placed to participate in activities.

number. Most friends had been met through clubs, day provision and when they moved to their homes in the community, or they were long-standing friends from hospital. Staff were also considered friends by some. Three-quarters reported having one or two friends among those who shared their home, and two-thirds had one or two friends living elsewhere. Only 11 per cent reported no contact with family, and only 4 per cent had no contact with friends.

Satisfaction with social contacts varied. Seven out of ten people saw enough of their friends who were co-residents, but only five out of ten saw enough of their friends living elsewhere. Dissatisfaction in this area stemmed from the desire for more, rather than less, contact. In fact, only 25 per cent were happy with the level of contact they had with their own families.

A small number of people had married since leaving hospital, or were about to marry. They tended to be older couples, and none had children. The marriages appear to have been comparatively settled, and no one had separated or divorced. Marriage required intensive support and counselling by staff, which was often forthcoming. Those who had married and participated in the study at five years often required staff support during the process of getting married or moving in together and after their marriage. Support was also needed for some other less conventional partnerships, some of them same-sex relationships. Help was also need for coming to terms with aspects of power and control in relationships, contraception and HIV and safer sex.

For one couple a flat was built alongside their hostel to give them added privacy and autonomy, while ensuring the level of support from staff which they continued to need. However, some other people found their relationships were not particularly well supported, and some staff or carers actively intervened in partnerships. Of course, it is difficult for staff to decide whether and how to intervene, particularly if a relationship is considered overtly abusive or detrimental to individual welfare in other ways. Even when abuse is obvious, the course of action is not necessarily predetermined, as issues of informed consent and confidentiality need to be carefully explored. For one couple the course chosen by staff was inaction, despite the risks and the negative impact on the entire household. For another couple, support was positive, staff recognising individuals' rights and providing counselling to help resolve the situation.

The nature of our data collection makes it impossible to make *direct* or simple comparisons of social contacts and relationships over time, but our contacts with people and services did suggest improvements over the years. Nevertheless, it is clear that there is a continuing need for community care agencies and carers to give emphasis to people's social networks.

Employment and income

Only 7 per cent of our sample had the opportunity to work with or without pay.
- Most of these people were involved in sheltered or supported work, or employed within the agency providing them with accommodation.
- One person was on employment training.
- Two people did voluntary work.
- One person had been working part-time in a canteen. His employers were so pleased with his work that they increased his hours, but not his wage.

As for many other people, the benefit trap kept earnings down, and no one earned a living wage. Although people were enthusiastic about their work which, among other things, gave them pride and a structure to the day, their part-time, unskilled, low-paid jobs ensured continued dependency on benefits. The same financial barriers also discouraged people from seeking jobs in the first place, for loss of benefits would jeopardise their accommodation.

The importance of benefit payments in the successful operation of community care needs to be stressed. Although care managers and keyworkers had helped people to claim their benefit entitlements, income from benefits was not always adequate to enable desired standards of support to be provided, let alone compensate for a paucity of social contacts, employment opportunities and personal belongings. This was sometimes the case even when social security benefits were supplemented by health service funding. At the time, there also remained the longstanding, nationwide problem of perverse incentives towards the use of residential care and nursing homes rather than domiciliary care settings (in order to take advantage of the higher social security entitlements), although this problem has been largely addressed by the community care reforms of April 1993. Whether the necessary supply response from domiciliary care and day activity providers will be forthcoming remains to be seen.

Personal presentation

Perception of an individual's appearance — the clothes they wear and their physical appearance generally — is defined and evaluated according to an existing cultural milieu. Social environments carry with them norms regarding appearance. People make assumptions about our personalities and social groups based on our clothes, physique, face, hair and other physical attributes. It is therefore important that people with learning disabilities are aware of and achieve relevant norms if community integration is to be successful and negative responses by others are to be avoided. Community care services face the perennial dilemma between intervening to improve or modify presentation and respecting the individual's right to self-determination.

Each user's personal presentation was noted during interviews. Users' clothing was not considered by interviewees to be 'unusual', but for one in ten it was particularly ill-fitting. A similar proportion wore dirty clothes (for example, with food stains), but only four people (3 per cent) expressed dissatisfaction with their clothes and possessions. In these various respects there were really no discernible differences between interviewers' views of personal presentation after one and five years in the community, or any differences between hospital and community.

The outcomes of community care

Since leaving hospital, the group of people with learning disabilities participating in this study had achieved many things. They had acquired new skills, made new friends (while also expressing a desire for more), taken up opportunities and had become more self-determining in activities and lifestyles. As indicated by their behavioural characteristics, they had largely coped well with the many challenges thrown up by these changes. They had not 'slipped through the net' of community provision.

However, most of the changes occurred during the first year in the community. In the subsequent four years, improvements were modest. Indeed, although some very good practices had been cemented in place, there were occasional warning signs that some community care services were in difficulty. There may simply be a ceiling to improvements in skills and other well-being dimensions. However, satisfaction levels expressed by individual service users remained high, even though access to employment and a decent level of income was still denied to them.

7 Services and Costs

The needs and welfare of people with learning disabilities are influenced by a wide range of factors. Community care aims to provide accommodation and appropriate assistance with the activities of daily living; it offers both generic and specialist services; it seeks to bring the skills and experiences of staff to the support of people whose disabilities and own lack of experience can leave them vulnerable. Clearly, it was important that the evaluation described accommodation, the services which people needed and/or used, and the associated costs. It was also important to explore the *links* between the characteristics of individual people, the services they received and the costs.

Service utilisation

During the original demonstration programme, each of the pilot projects had completed assessments of need for each person before they left hospital. Most of these assessments had been undertaken carefully and sensitively. Subsequently, through care management and service provision in the community, support agencies and carers endeavoured to keep abreast of changes in individual needs and preferences. And, within the ever-present resource and organisational constraints, these same agencies and carers had sought to respond to those needs by altering the patterns of service availability and receipt.

During interviews with users and staff we asked about service utilisation over the previous year. We also asked about unmet needs (see below). Numerous services were being used. Indeed, as Table 7.1 shows, 28 different services had been used at least once by more than 5 per cent of the full sample. Even though most people lived in specialist staffed care accommodation, it would be rare if not impossible (and probably inappropriate) for the achievement of good quality community support for every need to be met within the place of residence by facility-based staff. The data in the table refer to services which are *not* provided from accommodation budgets. (Thus some professional inputs, including some social worker or nursing support, day activity

Table 7.1
Service utilisation

Service received	Users %
In-patient hospital	14.6
Out-patient hospital	49.3
Day patient hospital	5.2
Day centre	54.0
Club	43.2
Social worker	31.0
GP	91.5
Chiropodist	48.4
Consultant	13.6
Dentist	60.6
Optician	43.7
Employment (or agency)	8.5
Education	50.2
Speech therapist	15.5
Psychologist	9.4
Physiotherapist	13.6
Nurse	28.6
Social security officer	8.0
Volunteer	22.1
Miscellaneous therapies/professions	23.0
Transport	7.5
Aids/adaptations	18.3
Holidays	9.9
Case review	37.6
Care management	10.3
Miscellaneous	7.5
Police	7.5
Home carer/help	8.0

Notes
a Sample size = 213.

programmes, holidays and generic supervisory 'overheads' which are part of an accommodation 'package' are not separately listed in the table.)

Some health services were heavily used. Fifteen per cent of the sample had been in-patients at some time during their fifth year in the community, compared to only 3 per cent during the first year after the original discharge from hospital (Knapp et al., 1992, Chap. 8). Most of these in-patient admissions had been prompted by physical health problems. A surprisingly large proportion of people (49 per cent) had used out-patient clinics, again mostly for physical health reasons, although some had attended psychiatric clinics. Again, this percentage was higher than the equivalent figure (34 per cent) four years earlier. One in seven people (14 per cent) had seen medical consultants outside the hospital setting, twice the proportion at the time of our previous research. Psychiatric consultations were often, but not always, simply for monitoring and medication checks.

Community-based health services had been used by almost everyone, including 92 per cent seeing a GP at least once (compared to 81 per cent after a year in the community), 61 per cent visiting a dentist (41 per cent four years earlier), and just under half receiving services from chiropodists and opticians. Less than a third had received nursing care, and only a few people lived in accommodation staffed by nurses. Levels of nursing input were the same after five years in the community as they were after one year. Nobody was using day patient facilities at the time of our last evaluation; now it was 5 per cent of the sample.

Day facilities, educational activities and social clubs had each been used by half the sample during the year, a similar proportion to that found four years earlier for these same people. These were usually segregated services for people with learning disabilities, such as social education centres and adult training centres, but most provided a structure appropriate to an ordinary life. Nine out of ten of the users we spoke to enjoyed going to day centres, and a similar proportion enjoyed the company of those they met there. Training in life skills and crafts was provided in education facilities, and some people pursued leisure activities in social clubs. As we reported earlier in the book, few people had found employment, and few centres provided a working routine (an exception being a garden centre open to the public).

Other services commonly used were (peripatetic) social work, volunteer support, aids and adaptations (such as incontinence pads and bathroom hoists), speech and various other therapies, and oral hygiene advice or treatment. There was only occasional use of hearing or music therapy, domestic support or counselling, and few people had contact with the police or received (new) social security assessments. Only a few people living in adult placements had used formal respite services.

How did service use compare after one and five years in the community? It is difficult to make comparisons over time because some of the former

pilot projects had initially established small 'generic' staff teams which provided a variety of support services, some of which had been disbanded before
our later evaluation. However, it was clear that health service utilisation had
increased considerably. This is partly an ageing effect. But it is also a reflection
of the high level of need for skilled medical care among people with learning
disabilities, a need which is generally not met from *within* community-based
accommodation settings. The utilisation rate for other services was the same
after five years as after one. 'Formal' community support had been maintained, even though the core services had moved out of the specially-funded
demonstration programme into the mainstream. However, as we describe in
the section on 'service needs and gaps', the availability of some support —
including inputs from social workers — did not appear to have kept pace
with need.

Leisure activities

Leisure activities are part of an ordinary and valued lifestyle. Some people
went to pubs and cafés on a regular basis. Although offering a community
presence, particularly when compared to opportunities in hospitals, pubs
and cafés do not necessarily ensure community participation, integration or
access to wider social networks. Similarly, clubs were often segregated so
that people with learning disabilities did not mix with people without disabilities. The exceptions provided additional opportunities for widening social
networks.

We asked individuals about their participation in activities and we assessed
the associated levels of satisfaction (which were very high). Many of the
activities listed in Table 7.2 took place in day facilities and training centres.
Although most people were active, only three-quarters felt that they had
enough to keep them occupied during the day. One in eight respondents
said they had too much to do, and one in five expressed dissatisfaction at
following the same routines every day.

Service needs and gaps

Although many services were used, staff reported a number of unmet needs
and service gaps. For the purposes of our interviews we defined *service needs*
as services that were necessary but not available, and a *service gap* as a deficit
in the use of, or provision by, any of the services utilised in the previous
year. Of course, staff perceptions of needs, gaps and associated barriers to
services were constructed within local contexts of service principles and
philosophies, and conditioned by the existence and knowledge of services.
Such influences could have been at least as important as their position in

Table 7.2

Participation in activities and user satisfaction

Activity	Percentage using	Percentage satisfied[a]	Sample size[b]
Industrial therapy	22	96	120
Occupational therapy	23	92	119
Art	50	100	137
Craft	56	100	99
Music	55	100	128
Drama	25	96	122
Clubs	56	95	128
Outings	70	100	93
Gardening	48	92	134
Housework	89	93	131
Cooking	71	99	132
Shopping	86	97	137
Laundry	78	95	102
Visiting	71	98	95

Notes

a Of those participating in the activity, the percentage who reported being satisfied with it.

b Number of people replying to each question.

relation to staff perceptions of user needs and individual service planning, although all possible services were described during the course of the interviews.

It was reported that about one in five of the sample were using education or training services that were felt to be inappropriate because of segregation, age inappropriateness or inadequate targeting. However, users did not generally report dissatisfaction. Staff perceptions of day support and clubs were similar: they were concerned that there was too much segregation, too little variety and inappropriate targeting, with providers sometimes underestimating users' abilities and ranges of interest, and consequently offering limited potential for development.

Some problems associated with hospital provision were identified by community-based staff, particularly a tendency for some specialists to ignore the user and address all questions to support staff, as well as the poor access more generally experienced in relation to medical or surgical opinions and interventions. Waiting times were criticised, particularly in emergencies or crises. More common than these complaints were criticisms about access to social work services. Almost one in ten respondents reported access difficulties, which they attributed to cutbacks, frozen posts, and the growth of other demands on social worker time. Among the most difficult services to

---

Access to mainstream services

In one London area there was a policy, shared across all agencies, to admit people with learning disabilities to hospital for the purposes of specialist treatment and not for long-term residence. One user was experiencing problems with her medication and a thorough review was sought. Instead of being conducted through primary health care, she was admitted to a distant mental handicap hospital for a month. When discharged she was found to have epilepsy.

Another user suffered from a leg infection and was admitted to hospital. There were serious problems with service coordination and, despite support workers maintaining daily contact, he was discharged from hospital without support or notice.

Confusion and isolation can be compounded by intellectual disability and by staff who are unskilled at recognising and responding to special needs, such as for communication.

---

access were some of the specialist therapies people needed, particularly speech therapy (used by one person in six).

A third of the sample were said to be in need of better support from volunteers who could act as advocates in facilitating community participation and integration. About a fifth of the sample were reported as having some volunteer support. Some users had been linked to volunteers for a time, but provision had often dropped off or ended abruptly. Those people who were still supported by a volunteer were not always satisfied with the contact, which could be irregular or occasional.

Overall, we identified high levels of unmet need and in some cases disturbing problems with existing provision. To fill these gaps and remedy these problems would require the introduction of new services, the extension or improvement of others, and better coordination. Most but not all would have resource implications. This is undoubtedly the task of community care planning, but links with formal assessment procedures are difficult to construct, especially when many authorities are aware of the legal issues in assessing unmet needs. While this is a task for individual service planning and care management at the individual level, there are potentially enormous implications for the resourcing of community care at the macro level and for the management of resources within care systems. There is not yet sufficient evidence to show whether community care planning or government funding will be robust enough or responsive enough to meet the changing demands within community care.

Table 7.3
Cost contributions

Service received	Average contributions to total cost %	Average cost per week Users only (£)	All people (£)
In-patient hospital	1.5	91.09	13.26
Out-patient hospital	0.6	4.89	2.41
Day patient hospital	0.1	15.66	0.81
Day centre	10.1	78.11	42.17
Club	0.2	1.55	0.67
Social worker	0.2	2.48	0.77
GP	0.2	1.16	1.06
Chiropodist	0.1	0.39	0.19
Consultant	–	1.28	0.17
Dentist	0.1	0.65	0.39
Optician	0.1	0.56	0.25
Employment (or agency)	0.3	20.24	1.71
Education	1.4	15.22	7.65
Speech therapist	0.2	9.03	1.40
Psychologist	–	2.47	0.23
Physiotherapist	0.2	10.16	1.38
Nurse	0.5	6.84	1.96
Social security officer	–	0.31	0.03
Volunteer	0.3	7.30	1.61
Misc. therapies/professions	0.2	5.07	1.17
Transport	0.1	5.07	0.38
Aids/adaptations	0.1	4.21	0.77
Holidays	0.1	3.37	0.33
Case review	0.2	3.45	1.29
Care management	–	0.95	0.98
Miscellaneous	0.1	3.77	0.28
Police	-	0.28	0.21
Home carer/help	0.1	8.78	0.70

Notes

a Sample size = 213

b '–' indicates that the percentage was greater than zero but less than 0.05.

Table 7.4
Total costs over time

Place of accommodation five years after leaving hospital[a]	Weekly costs (£, mid-1992 price levels)			
	In hospital £	After 1 year in community £	After 5 years in community £	N
Residential home	552	515	491	17
Hostel	550	475	546	33
Sheltered housing	427	601	687	16
Staffed group home	527	697	687	62
Unstaffed group home	492	620	472	13
Adult placement	475	613	450	9
Independent living	433	572	495	6
Hospital	551	397	1028	1
Unclassified	452	557	450	2
All accommodation types	514	602	598	159

Note

a Place of accommodation refers to five years after hospital discharge only. Initially everyone was in hospital, and placements after one year were different from those after five years for many people.

Costs

Costs were calculated for each of the services which people had used (the most common of them listed in Table 7.1). Services were costed at their long-run marginal opportunity costs. By *opportunity cost* we mean that the resource implications should reflect opportunities forgone rather than amounts spent (when this information is available). By *marginal* we mean the addition to total cost attributable to the inclusion of one more service user. By *long-run* we mean to move beyond the costs of using present services more intensively to examine the costs of creating new services to meet the demands of the future substitution of community support for long-term hospital care (Knapp, 1993; Beecham, 1994).

Summary cost information is given in Table 7.3 for the services most frequently used in the community. The table shows the high percentage use but low contribution to total cost of certain key services, such as general practice and community nursing. However, the services listed in this table account for only 17 per cent of total cost. Most of the remainder — the lion's share of the cost of community care — is accounted for by accommodation, including living expenses and staff employed on site, within facility budgets.

Although a high proportion of total cost falls to the accommodation budget, with much of the formal support which people need being provided within

Figure 7.1
Costs trends over time

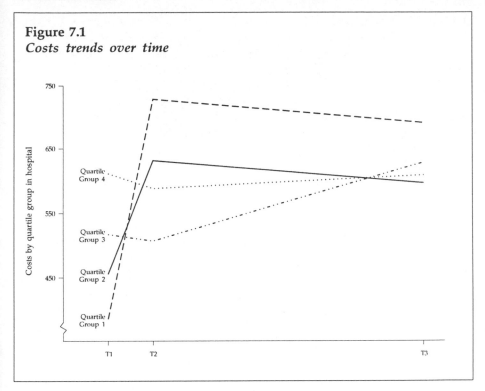

their place of residence, community care clearly has implications for many other agencies and budgets. With such a multiplicity of services there are always dangers of fragmentation of responsibilities, gaps in the responsiveness of services to needs, and cost shunting. These problems are being tackled by the community care reforms, although they will not easily be overcome in some localities (Wistow et al., 1994). The former pilot projects, of course, had been set up to tackle some of these difficulties, and their strategic organisation of joint working between health and social services authorities, and in some cases also some voluntary organisations, helped to reduce the likelihood of gaps and conflicts (see Chapter 8). The introduction of individual programme planning and care management in many areas helped to translate these strategic aims into good practice with individual users (Chapter 9).

The aggregate weekly costs of community care are given in Table 7.4, arranged by type of accommodation. For the 159 people for whom we had data over the full research period of more than five years, average cost per week after five years in the community was £598 (at mid-1992 price levels).

With the exception of hospital in-patient readmissions, aggregate costs were highest for people living in smaller settings (especially staffed group homes and sheltered housing), but nowhere were they particularly low. Table 7.4 also gives the weekly costs in hospital prior to the move to the community which marked inclusion in the Care in the Community programme and after one year in the community. These costs are arranged by accommodation placement after five years. (For example, the one person in hospital at the time of the five-year interviews had a weekly cost of £1,028. Four years earlier, they were living in *community* accommodation, with costs of £397.) The comparisons over time reveal that average costs after five years in the community were virtually the same as after one year (when they were £602 per week). Compared to hospital, however, the long-term cost of community care — after the initial relocation difficulties have been overcome, when new services have settled down, and users and care managers have been able to tailor service packages to needs — is very much greater: £598 per week after five years in the community, compared to £514 per week in hospital.

These broad averages hide some important interpersonal cost variations. If we group people by their costs when in hospital we can trace costs over time (Figure 7.1). (The groups distinguished in this figure are defined by the distribution of costs in hospital. Group 1 comprises people whose hospital costs were below the first quartile: they were the 'lowest-cost 25 per cent' at that time. These groups are not the same as those defined in order to illustrate trends in skills and behaviour in Figures 6.1 and 6.2.) The group with the lowest costs in hospital subsequently received the most costly community care, although not too much should be read into this trend, for the intergroup differences are not significant in the community.

From one perspective, it is perhaps not surprising that aggregate costs have changed relatively little over time, given the dominance of accommodation within total cost and the difficulties which health and local authorities have experienced in making new and perhaps less costly community accommodation and other facilities available. In addition, as we described in the previous chapter, people acquired few new self-care skills after the initial year in the community and still had a number of behaviour problems. They therefore continued to need staff support and assistance in many aspects of their lives.

It is reassuring that the totality of service responses to people's needs appears to have held up despite loss of special 'project' status, in particular the withdrawal of central government special funds, sometimes without the local public sector agencies replacing them with the local funds which they had promised. There were also a number of other developments (see Chapter 8). However, there have been some changes in the level and pattern of service utilisation. Earlier we noted the marked increase in use of some health services. Experience of in-patient admissions, for example, increased from 3 per cent of the sample to 15 per cent, although the average duration of each admission was much shorter (as reflected in the cost difference: an average per week *over the fifth year* of £91, less than half the equivalent figure for the first year).

The proportion of the sample using day activities outside the accommodation setting (including social clubs) was roughly the same in the first and fifth years, as was the *amount* used (averaging £80 per week for users), but there had been a big change in relation to education. The same proportion of people (50 per cent) were making some use of this service, but the amount of educational support was much lower (average weekly costs fell from £72 to £15 for those people using the service). Whether this reduction is fully justified by the improved abilities of people (particularly in relation to the acquisition of or improvement of self-care skills during the first year in the community) is open to debate. Another cost reduction over time — again consistent with findings described earlier in the chapter — was in relation to community social care services (outside the accommodation setting or budget), where average weekly cost across the full sample fell from £18 in the first year of community care to £5 in the fifth year.

Costs, needs and outcomes

The lowest cost package of support for someone in our sample was £167 per week, compared with the highest cost of £1097 per week. What accounts for this variation? A number of factors can be hypothesised to lie behind differences in cost (Knapp, 1994), including the needs-related and other characteristics of individual people, the type of accommodation in which they live, key features of the support services used, and the style of care management.

One of the questions to be asked of community care is whether packages of support respond effectively to differences in individual need. Costs are useful as summary measures of provision since they combine all formal services used, including accommodation, and employ the same unit of measurement (money) to sum them.

We examined the link between costs and the characteristics of individuals when they were in hospital. Multiple regression analysis was used to explore the power of these individual characteristics in the prediction of costs after five years in the community. The results can be summarised by the equation in Table 7.5 which — like the multiple regression equations for skills and behaviour described in the previous chapter — is the final analysis of a series, and combines parsimony with statistical significance and interpretability. The analysis shows that 42 per cent of the cost variation can be 'explained' statistically by the characteristics individuals more than five years early. This is quite a high correlation for such a time elapse. (It is slightly better than that found in equivalent work in relation to former psychiatric hospital residents; Knapp et al., 1990, 1994.) This correlation is testament to two things: the targeting of community support services on previously assessed needs, and the continuity and stability of the major cost elements in the community, notably accommodation.

The cost-raising influences of the skills and behaviour characteristics in Table 7.5 have two interpretations. Some indicate a *need effect*: people with

Table 7.5
Cost predictions after five years from skills and behaviour characteristics in hospital

Explanatory variables (skills and behaviour in hospital[a])	β	Sig.
Constant term	554.70	.000
Conversation, social mixing — only with prompting	-87.01	.005
Non-verbal community — normal	-102.76	.001
Washing and bathing self — adequate without supervision	-163.86	.000
Shopping ability — adequate with supervision	56.64	.058
Individual has missed opportunities to participate in activities	77.19	.021
Writing ability — few words only	-100.00	.023
Underactivity — all or most of the time	-93.01	.025
Attention-seeking behaviour — none or only mild problem	-123.81	.000
Collecting, hoarding meaningless items — no problem	97.39	.012
Incontinence at night — none	-74.26	.060
Wanders or runs away — rarely or never	158.20	.002
Sample size	112	
R^2 and $\bar{R}^2$	0.42	0.35
F and significance	6.58	.000

Notes

a All explanatory variables except skills and behaviour scores are 'dummy variables', taking the value 1 if an individual has the listed characteristic and the value 0 otherwise.

lower levels of ability in relation to certain skills or greater behavioural problems require more support on a daily basis. This is the reason for the links between cost and non-verbal communication, washing and bathing, missing opportunities to participate in activities, writing ability, attention-seeking behaviour and incontinence. People facing difficulties in these areas need more staff or carer support. A different interpretation can be placed on the other influences. People who previously had low skills in relation to conversation and social mixing, and shopping, or who were described as being underactive all or most of the time, are now receiving care or support 'packages' which are *less* costly than those used by people without these characteristics. This may be due to the fact that it is members of the latter group who are encouraged by staff to participate in a wide range of activities, especially outside the home. This may also be the reason why people who did not have a problem with wandering or running away are receiving more comprehensive support packages. This *activity effect* is different from the 'need effect', though both can push up costs.

We also examined whether the cost differences between accommodation types (reported in Table 7.4) persisted after standardising for those individual skills and behavioural characteristics significantly associated with costs (Table 7.5). We conducted analyses of variance of residual ('unexplained') costs against accommodation type and sector. Other things being equal, costs were significantly lower in more independent settings (adult placements, supporting lodgings, independent living), and were significantly greater than expected costs, relative to users' characteristics when assessed in hospital, in sheltered housing and staffed group homes.

In further examinations we found costs to be related to a number of 'project' or locality characteristics, particularly aspects of the micro- and macro-organisation of community care. However, these were difficult to interpret and are not reported here.

Finally, we broadened the examination of cost differences by considering the simple links between costs and outcomes, the latter defined as changes in the skills and behaviour characteristics of individuals between the one-year and five-year interviews, complementing the statistical analyses reported in the previous chapter. We found no links between costs and outcomes.

Support services and responsibilities

We have seen that the people with learning disabilities participating in this study received support from a wide variety of services, although they were not able to gain access to everything which they or staff felt they needed, and some of the services received were not as well planned or delivered as they wanted.

Although average aggregate support costs after five years in the community were similar to costs after one year, the *composition* of the community support packages had changed in significant ways. There was, for example, a much smaller educational input, and social work and other community social care services were not as readily available as keyworkers thought necessary, and the amounts being accessed were considerably lower than had been the case four years earlier. As well as these declining rates of utilisation and levels of usage (and some other service gaps), we found a number of problems with inappropriately or inadequately targeted services.

When we looked at links between service utilisation, as measured in summary form by cost and individual characteristics in hospital, we found some fairly strong connections. These links between needs and services, and the general coordination of services, were often among the responsibilities of care management, to which we now turn.

8 Organising and Managing Community Care

In the period since the people in our study moved from hospital, there have been enormous changes in the organisation and management of health and community care. As we described in Chapter 2, among the many implications of the 1990 NHS and Community Care Act have been the realignment of agency roles and responsibilities in pursuit of better coordination of service responses to needs and the further encouragement of the mixed economy of care. Although the final stages of the community care reforms were not implemented until April 1993, earlier changes certainly left their mark on the services covered by our research. In a few cases, complex feedback loops operated from central policy initiative to the pilot services, back to central policy-making via the Audit Commission and the Social Services Inspectorate and back again to intervene in the twelve projects. We pick up on these interconnections in more detail in the next chapter. However, project experience helped close the implementation gap between central policy and local service management and organisation.

In some cases the impact was seemingly marginal or indirect, for instance changing the provider of a single service, or changing the funding route. When this happened quickly it left some staff and users feeling vulnerable. These changes reinforced the need for someone to be responsible for safeguarding each user's interests, working across agency and sector boundaries in order to assess needs, coordinate services and monitor progress. Care management of this kind was, of course, a precondition of the initial central government funding of each of the former demonstration projects, generally giving them a head start in tailoring case-level organisation to local circumstances. Since then both the function and nature of care management have developed in many of the twelve areas, as we explore more fully in the next chapter.

The reforms are creating new opportunities through the commissioning process, from their emphasis on comprehensive joint assessment and the requirement to take account of users' preferences in reaching decisions, to the encouragement of greater competition between providers and the more searching monitoring of quality and efficiency. It will be recalled that another condition for DHSS grant funding of pilot projects was the establishment of good joint working relationships between health and social services authorities. This was achieved in different ways and with varying degrees of success across the original demonstration programme (Knapp et al., 1992, Chap. 11).

With their origins as jointly funded ventures, most projects retained some level of joint commissioning or pooled budgets through joint health and social services involvement. In Maidstone, in Kent, this was at the interagency and divisional levels, but with purchasing through care management, so that the level of joint commissioning within organisations varied. The absence of joint commissioning can lead to confusion over funding responsibilities, as in Camden. Both of these examples will be described below. Our earlier work illustrated that some services were moving towards brokerage arrangements at the individual and agency levels and had developed joint or lead agency care management teams (see Cambridge, 1992, for organisational typology) thus moving towards joint individual service specifications (Cambridge, 1992), based upon an agreed mission (Knapp and Wistow, 1993), although only in the Maidstone service were contracts the end product of this process.

Over time, some authorities began to question the viability of these jointly managed projects as integral services in newly emerging care markets (see Figure 8.1), and instead favoured transferring the provider role to the voluntary or private sectors, with public agencies concentrating on commissioning. Once again, therefore, some of the projects were introducing organisational arrangements locally which later became national policy. Today in many parts of the country, health and social services authorities are introducing or exploring joint commissioning as a major element of interagency collaboration. Many have sought their first joint commissioning ventures in relation to services for people with learning disabilities living in the community (Wertheimer and Greig, 1993).

National developments in community care policy have therefore brought about a number of organisational and practice changes in the localities in which the former Care in the Community projects are found. In this chapter we describe some of the changes in two localities — Camden and Somerset — which illustrate quite contrasting experiences. We then explore more fully the links between macro- and micro-organisation in Chapter 9, particularly concentrating on care management experiences across the twelve areas. In this cae, Maidstone provides an interesting example.

Developments in Camden

In common with many other service contexts, the macro-organisation of care in Camden was complex (Figure 8.2). CSMH housing service — a voluntary organisation — took on the management of the Living in Camden (LinC)

Figure 8.1
Changing macro-organisational environment

Traditional joint-working arrangements

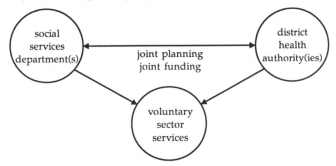

New inter-agency working

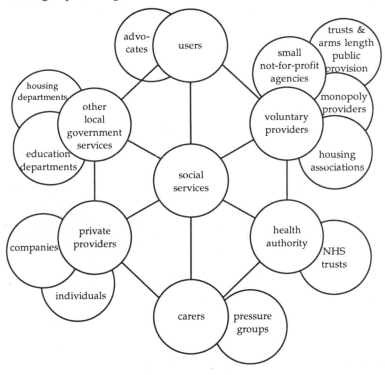

Figure 8.2
Macro-organisation in Camden

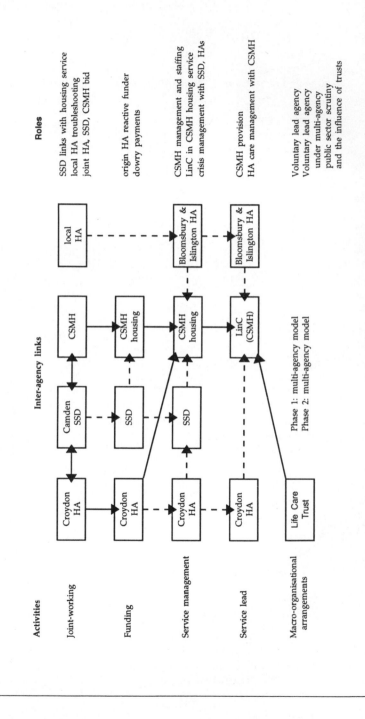

Activities	Inter-agency links				Roles
Joint-working	Croydon HA ↔ Camden SSD ↔ CSMH				SSD links with housing service local HA troubleshooting joint HA, SSD, CSMH bid
Funding	Croydon HA → CSMH housing SSD				origin HA reactive funder dowry payments
Service management	Croydon HA → SSD → CSMH housing ← Bloomsbury & Islington HA				CSMH management and staffing LinC in CSMH housing service crisis management with SSD, HAs
Service lead	Croydon HA → LinC (CSMH) ← Bloomsbury & Islington HA				CSMH provision HA care management with CSMH
Macro-organisational arrangements	Life Care Trust → LinC (CSMH) Phase 1: multi-agency model Phase 2: multi-agency model				Voluntary lead agency Voluntary lead agency under multi-agency public sector scrutiny and the influence of trusts

project at the request of the London Borough of Camden Social Services Department and Croydon Health Authority. The aim was to help people who lived at the then St Lawrence's Hospital at Caterham, and who were originally from Camden, to return to the Borough in a planned and well-supported way. The project offered:

- community-based support staff using 'getting-to-know-you' techniques to work with people with learning disabilities and their relatives in preparing the way for a return to community living;
- a flexible service with an individual needs-based approach;
- the direct provision of support for personal needs, practical living skills and advice and counselling;
- encouragement for people to use ordinary services and facilities offered in Camden and throughout London;
- help in maintaining existing relationships with family and friends and in developing new relationships; and
- the provision of support for daytime activities.

The housing management function for the LinC project aimed to offer a local housing service which valued the person with a learning disability as a full citizen with individual rights and responsibilities, adhering to the principle that houses were homes for life, if that was what the service user wanted. Management responsibility for the LinC project was shared with Camden Social Services during the first eighteen months of operation.

Achieving these principles for a group of users, many of whom had physical disabilities or challenging behaviours, proved expensive. The costs of the service increased beyond the level of funding agreed with Croydon Health Authority. Moreover, CSMH did not have the organisational capacity or competence to deal with the resulting financial crisis. The local coordinating and funding agencies distanced themselves from the growing problems of CSMH. In April 1991 St Lawrence's Hospital became the Lifecare Trust (a new NHS provider unit). There were financial and organisational disincentives for Croydon Health Authority, Bloomsbury and Islington Health Authority, Lifecare NHS Trust and the London Borough of Camden to become directly involved and there were few commonly shared interests.

The difficulties confronting LinC had a knock-on effect on the credibility of CSMH, particularly serious at a time when the LinC Project represented only about a third of CSMH's operational capacity. Until April 1991 CSMH had pursued a policy of subsidising the costs of the LinC project from other sources of income. This policy became untenable as the deficit in funding continued to grow, placing the entire organisation at risk. At its peak, the accumulated debts of CSMH amounted to around £400,000, due entirely to the losses made by the LinC project. To address the problem, CSMH carried out major restructuring of its housing provision and negotiated a substantial increase in the level of funding for users with complex and expensive support needs.

Beyond the potentially devastating local effect of any collapse of CSMH, there were also implications for the future role and status of voluntary providers of community care. With voluntary organisations involved as lead agencies in providing or managing care for people with learning disability, the experience of CSMH was unlikely to be unique.

Most residents originating from Camden left St Lawrence's in 1987, although three had moved out in 1985. Croydon Health Authority agreed to pay CSMH £13,000 per person, stemming from its original responsibility for St Lawrence's Hospital, and seventeen residents became users of the LinC project. The dowries were relatively low, standing at £14,840 by 1991. Croydon Health Authority had appeared to be unhappy about the level of funding going out of the authority, and considered the LinC project a Rolls Royce service. This policy had allowed Croydon to spend a proportionately higher amount on hospital reprovision within its own area. The hospital and its associated resettlement service were involved in working with LinC to assist the discharge of Camden users, but with NHS Trust status the hospital adopted a more independent stance. Lifecare Trust also had experience in managing hospital reprovision schemes through a housing service in Croydon, a replacement service and a specialist day resource in the borough. The trust retained an interest in the LinC users through its resettlement service which followed up and monitored users, although the regularity of contact fluctuated.

The Trust readmitted three Camden users to its hospital service as an indirect result of the financial difficulties faced by CSMH. One was readmitted in 1987 and the others in 1991. The lack of individualised funding meant that CSMH was unable to afford the provision of a service to these users, all of whom had relatively intensive support needs as a result of their challenging behaviours. In May 1991 CSMH asked for joint assessments to be carried out by Lifecare Trust and Bloomsbury and Islington Health Authority, with a view to establishing the support needs and associated service costs of the LinC users. These would also help determine the real cost of the service which CSMH was providing and aid the rationalisation of the loss-making LinC project which CSMH had committed itself to undertaking in its 1991/92 Business Plan.

Two people were readmitted to St Lawrence's Hospital following complaints from neighbours about noise and disturbance, and subsequent legal action against CSMH. This resulted in an out-of-court settlement, as CSMH could not risk losing in the High Court and being found in contempt. This would have resulted in a rolling programme of repeated fines and liability for costs. The case cost CSMH financially and cost the two users their right to live in the community. Other users also bore the brunt of under- funding, as efforts to cut revenue expenditure and maximise receipts meant reducing the number of void places, and moving away from models of intensive support in small-scale settings. At the expense of ensuring more people were not readmitted to hospital, some of principles of the service, such as needs-based work and user consultation, were compromised. Some users had to move house.

By April 1991 senior managers in CSMH had become aware of the dilemma facing the organisation and developed alternative strategies which would finally resolve the issue, either restructuring the service and its provision with increased funding, or closing the service down with users probably being readmitted to hospital.

> Since the inception of the LinC project in 1985, CSMH had difficulty in coming to terms with the reality of not having sufficient funds to provide the type of housing service reflected in its stated values ... CSMH cannot continue to provide a service that it cannot afford (CSMH Business Plan April 1991-March 1992).

A better understanding of the issues facing CSMH from other organis-ational players and increasing pressure from funders, creditors and senior members of staff within CSMH led to the resignation of the director and managers of the housing service. The implementation of the 1991/92 Business Plan meant substantial changes to working conditions for staff, and — without an increase in funding from Croydon Health Authority — the possibility of redundancy.

From interviews with staff during this period it was clear that most were very concerned about the future of the people with learning disabilities whom they supported and for their own jobs. Morale was low and changes in working practices and hours were imposed. For example, poor attendance at work resulted in lower pay, and redundancy notices were issued and withdrawn while negotiating increased funding from Croydon. Changes in the terms and conditions of staff working in the housing service included the introduction of overtime payments, restructuring rotas, limiting the num-ber of staff on annual leave at any one time, negotiations to limit employee sick leave (later abandoned), an increase in the working week from 35 to 36 hours, regrading salaries to correspond with the introduction of allowances for weekend and bank holiday working, and associated changes in manage-ment roles, grades and posts. There was also an increase to the establishment of housing administration and finance, the closure of an office building and tighter controls on expenditure and rent arrears.

In order to present their argument that the service was underfunded, CSMH commissioned the first real assessments of user needs since people had left hospital. They also undertook a series of restructuring proposals for the organisation of the housing service to meet the individual needs of each user where possible (*Internal Report on the Housing Restructuring Process — Stage Two*). The proposals included different possible groupings of users and properties by keyworkers and teams. The conclusion was an average cost of £30,000 a year for supporting the former LinC users. In August 1991 CSMH notified Croydon Health Authority of its deadline for an increase in the funding necessary to avoid the close-down of the service. Croydon initially refused any increase and issued a press statement saying they were prepared to readmit people to hospital. After a short but intensive media campaign conducted by CSMH, which highlighted the anomaly of Croydon's position, funding was increased to £30,000 per person. Due to the effective restructuring of housing provision no increase to this amount was sought in April 1992, and no more people were readmitted to hospital.

The service provided to the former residents of St Lawrence's Hospital has emerged from these difficulties more robust and stable, with a greater emphasis on quality outcomes and overall performance. The organisation has used the experience to develop new styles of service delivery which reflect more closely the expectation of an ordinary life for all. However, instability and fragmentation remain ever-present challenges in the evolving community care environment.

Learning from the Camden experience

How is experience in Camden relevant to community care more generally? It is evident that the crisis confronting CSMH was confounded by a number of factors which services and commissioners can work to avoid or reduce

- *Inadequate service performance monitoring within and outside CSMH.* Poor information was available on service performance, in particular on individual service costs and outcomes. CSMH was not skilled or resourced to undertake proper assessments and reviews or develop individual service planning.
- *Lack of a positive and collective working culture.* Pressurised community workers and crisis management did not enable CSMH effectively to stake a claim for available resources. Under threat of closure and redundancies, the service was divided internally, with support staff and management unsupportive of each other.
- *Lack of locally coordinated community care planning.* The signs from Camden do not suggest that community care planning will easily or pain-lessly overcome diverse and sometimes competing organisational interests or the divisions in organisational and funding responsibilities found in community care.
- *Lack of an integrated local service strategy.* Specialist challenging needs services were developed by CSMH (with health authority funding) through its Goldhurst Project. These provide training, support and individual pro-grammes around challenging behaviour. Many community services lack such specialist resources and expertise, as part of a strategy including early detection, prevention and longer-term support.

- *Confusion over responsibilities for care management and service coordination.* The 1990 reforms refer to the potential role of care management for people with complex or expensive needs. CSMH did not have the resources to develop care management. Interventions from Lifecare Trust and Bloomsbury and Islington Health Authority took over this role, but there was little continuity over time.
- *Poorly defined accountability.* There was little accountability within CSMH or to funders, resulting in periods of crisis management. This was partly a consequence of confusion over responsibilities and resources between agencies. There were unrealistic expectations made of a voluntary organisation lacking the technical and financial expertise found in the statutory sector.

A number of more general transferable lessons are also provided by the experience of CSMH. Effective community care needs the following:

- *Agreements allocating responsibilities, founded on a shared value base and expectations for service performance, including quality and costs.* Contracts alone, particularly when arranged around individual services, such as through devolved care management budgets, are unlikely to provide the medium- and longer-term stability required for service development, including training.
- *Effective monitoring by social services and other purchasers.* It is optimistic to expect service commissioning and a mixed economy of community care to clarify accountability to users or taxpayers. Special arrangements may need to be developed through care management, advocacy or special community watchdog resources. Alternatively, the responsibilities of local auditors or inspectorates may need to be extended.
- *An understanding of the relationships between needs, resources and outcomes.* This will be helped by devolved budgets and care management, but will require management information systems covering individual service utilisation, unmet needs and costs, linked with resource allocation and service planning at the macro level to help tackle inequities.
- *Strong and confident leadership.* This is needed to manage constructively the tensions between individual and organisational needs and outcomes. With voluntary providers coming under increasing pressure, it will be essential to have skilled and confident leadership to navigate organisations from crisis management to planned service development.
- *Constructive partnerships between interested agencies focused on the needs of users.* This will require careful community care planning which engages the diverse interests of providers, purchasers and users. The current arrangements are more like enhanced joint planning. In locations like Camden, where boundaries cross and agency responsibilities are unclear, the challenges are considerable.

Figure 8.3
Line management levels in Somerset's care and case management structure

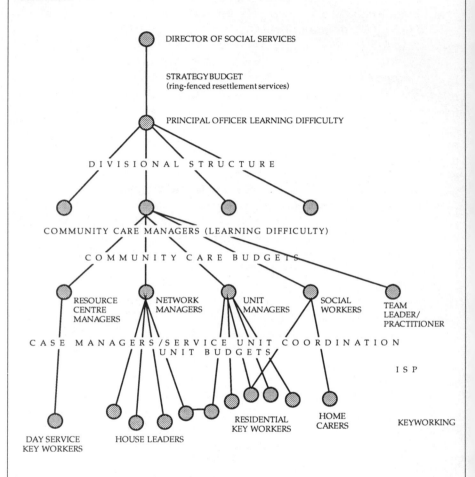

DIRECTOR OF SOCIAL SERVICES

STRATEGY BUDGET
(ring-fenced resettlement services)

PRINCIPAL OFFICER LEARNING DIFFICULTY

D I V I S I O N A L   S T R U C T U R E

COMMUNITY CARE MANAGERS (LEARNING DIFFICULTY)

C O M M U N I T Y   C A R E   B U D G E T S

RESOURCE CENTRE MANAGERS

NETWORK MANAGERS

UNIT MANAGERS

SOCIAL WORKERS

TEAM LEADER/ PRACTITIONER

C A S E   M A N A G E R S / S E R V I C E   U N I T   C O O R D I N A T I O N
U N I T   B U D G E T S

I S P

DAY SERVICE KEY WORKERS

HOUSE LEADERS

RESIDENTIAL KEY WORKERS

HOME CARERS

KEYWORKING

USERS
self-advocacy

PEOPLE FIRST
facilitated self-advocacy groups

- *A strategic and shared approach to funding community services, focused on the needs of users.* This will require creative agreements for resourcing services, responsive to considerations of equity and access for individual users. It will also need to provide some level of protected funding.

Lead agency developments in Somerset

In the early 1980s in Somerset, the social services department took on lead responsibility for managing and providing housing and day support services for people with a learning disability in the county. This lead role was designed around a joint strategy developed with Somerset Health Authority for the movement of over 400 people from three hospitals (Sandhill Park near Taunton, Norah Fry in Shepton Mallet and Selwood in Frome) to new community services. The health authority was the purchaser. The strategy budget in Somerset effectively provided protected funds for community services for people with learning disabilities, and was subsequently devolved to four community care managers at divisional level (there are also community care managers for other client groups).

The divisional structure represented a reorganisation away from fieldwork areas in response to the management demands of the strategy and the community care reforms. Community care management at divisional level enabled Somerset to tackle questions of equity and target efficiency, particularly addressing the needs of people who had not moved out of hospital. In some other localities special care in the community resources have resulted in the development of two-tier services.

Somerset recognised early on that they needed to develop a care-managed approach in order to target services on needs and to have the information required for billing the health authority for services provided under the strategy budget. In Somerset a user's care manager is a social worker, manager of a residential network, unit or resource centre, team leader or practitioner, depending on the type of residential provision and other aspects of the service package. The care manager is responsible for service coordination, individual service planning (ISP) and review. Reviews are attended by users, advocates, relatives and keyworkers, and are designed to integrate different service components, such as residential and day support services.

Service coordination in Somerset is facilitated by in-house service management and provision, integrated in each division, with access to information systems on individual service utilisation, needs and associated costs (Figure 8.3). Community care managers are included in reviews where there are significant resource implications. Frameworks for ISP and case review are provided, but scope is retained for developing local responses, such as the assessment tools used and intervals for review. As such, the Somerset arrange-

---

Box 8.1
The opportunities and risks in an emerging community care market

Opportunities	Risks
• more choice for purchasers and service users	• service fragmentation and loss of strategy
• efficient division of responsibilities between agencies	• wasteful duplication and rivalry
• innovation and creativity	• diminishing public accountability
• devolved authority and budgets	• inequalities and inequities in redistributing resources
• developing quality and cost-effective services	• putting cost and savings before quality
• efficient management and information systems	• raiding resources from direct provision
• constructive consultation and cooperation	• confrontation between commissioners and providers
• partnership between providers	• monopoly and duopoly provision
• contracts define responsibilities and expectations	• short-termism creates instability and uncertainties
• consensus between purchasers and providers	• special interest alliances exclude users

---

ments combine a lead agency model with shared core task arrangements, as defined in the care management and assessment guide (DH/SSI, 1991a).

Lead provision by the social services department may not be fashionable, but is an appropriate organisational response in many places where there is not a ready market in residential care or other services for people with learning disabilities. Somerset has chosen to go slowly down the road of developing a mixed economy, avoiding options such as trusts or consortia in the medium term. In geographically widespread services, where there is no variety of genuine choices, this often has to be the medium-term strategy if well-integrated and equitable services are a political or organisational objective. As one social services manager explained:

> The strategy is such a huge process of change, that momentum has to be maintained without waiting for markets to emerge. The whole basis of the strategy demands that we create services that people need, where and when they need them. ... There may be an argument for putting some resources at arm's length, but we would have to look at a number of different consortia to generate any real choice.

The availability of joint finance enabled the authority to cope with the higher than anticipated 'double-funding' costs of the strategy. There were originally ten 'core houses' planned, but after the development of those in

Taunton, Bridgwater, Yeovil and Frome there was a reappraisal of their function, and the core and cluster model evolved into a more flexible network model. This also helped cut development costs at a time when the service was experiencing higher levels of user dependency than anticipated, and enabled day support services to be developed into non-segregated community resources.

Organisational lessons

The CSMH experience in Camden points to the dangers of an implementation gap between central and local community care policy and practice. It has highlighted issues of accountability, both contractually and to local people and users. Provision which is moved out of the public sector or which operates in a quasi-independent mode can become remote from local interests. One interpretation of events was that CSMH bore the brunt of a newly emerging care market where the roles and powers of participating agencies were being tested for the first time. Whether or not this is a valid view, the events illustrate some of the opportunities and risks inherent in a market approach to community care (see Box 8.1).

This can be compared with the situation in Somerset, where there are more or less integrated community services for people with learning disabilities. Service objectives are shared between the major public sector organisations — the funders and providers of community care. Agency roles and responsibilities are clearer, and services are more likely to be planned and developed according to agreed strategies. In principle, there is the organisational capacity and competence to respond to changing political and financial conditions, with accountability through members, to the local electorate. Services are designed around the needs of individuals, with accumulating knowledge of the relationships between resources and outcomes. There was no ready care market for learning disability services in Somerset, and options for diversifying provision were carefully explored.

There is some evidence that the government's community care reforms are helping to polarise services and interests in the organisation and practice of community care with the risk of increasing inequities in resource allocation and access. Joint commissioning is helping to identify gaps and overlaps in local services by developing common procedures for determining service priorities and patterns of provision. The future direction, form and ultimate success of a more mixed economy of community care will hinge as much on local interpretations, priorities and behaviour as on national policy objectives. Although there is less of a mixed economy in Somerset than in Kent, we will see in the next chapter how the two authorities contrast in their roles of lead agency as provider and lead agency as enabling authority.

9 Care Management

The successes of the early British care management experiments in Kent and elsewhere led the Audit Commission (1986, 1987) to recommend care management as a key component of community care reform. Griffiths (1988) recommended that care managers carry responsibility for budget-holding, and the 1989 White Paper, *Caring for People*, saw merit in nominating a care manager where 'an individual's needs are complex or significant levels of resources are involved'.

In planning community services for people leaving hospital during the demonstration programme phase, each of the twelve pilot projects had to address some basic care management questions, including:

- how to make individual service planning an integral part of the service;
- how to take account of the preferences of users and carers in individual and group service plans; and
- how to allocate responsibility for service plans, review of progress and resource allocation.

In projects with well-designed infrastructures, the knowledge and understanding needed to answer these and related questions was partly derived from information about individual needs, in the context of the local strategic organisation of community care (see Chapter 8). This user-specific information should stem from competent staff support and keyworking practices, and should feed into individual service planning. ISP is one of the core tasks of care management, the others being: case finding and referral; assessment, screening and selection; monitoring, review and reassessment; and case closure (Challis and Davies, 1986). The local responses to the organisational challenges raised by these core tasks had implications for the targeting of resources, user participation, accountability and cost-effectiveness.

Variations of the core tasks have appeared in other definitions or interpretations of care management, such as 'the movement of each individual client from application status to case closure' (Henke et al., 1975), and in the 1989 White Paper *Caring for People*. Although care management is a process, it is also a function. It is easy to appreciate care management as 'the lynch-pin of an individual needs-led service' (Audit Commission, 1989) and our preferred definition would be 'the organisation of information, resources and worker responsibility around the needs and wants of individual service users'.

There has been confusion about the use of the terms case and care management. Griffiths (1988) introduced the latter term. The Department of Health has switched between case and care management (compare *Caring for People* with the care management and assessment guides for managers and practitioners). We will consistently use the term care management, although case management emphasises an individual focus and is more widely understood in an international context (although users are not 'cases' to be 'managed').

Markets in Maidstone

Care management originated in North America where it was considered necessary to safeguard the interests of users in a multiagency market. Starting as a form of professional advocacy, it evolved into service brokerage with individualised funding. Early British models, which were developed in relation to support services for elderly people in parts of Kent, devolved budgets to case managers (as they were then called). Painstaking research had found that the new care management arrangements produced better user outcomes for elderly people at lower costs (Challis and Davies, 1986).

The Maidstone Care in the Community pilot project provided an opportunity to replicate these earlier care management experiments in another part of the county, for the project's architects saw these arrangements as likely to prove helpful for managing the movement of people and resources between hospital and community services. In the longer term, following the 1990 Act and the recommendations of management consultants, this budgeting arrangement did not prove sustainable alongside the systemic introduction of care management in Kent. Although experience in Maidstone helped inform the county-wide design of care management as a purchasing device and for involving users, its largely experimental design was overtaken by changing national policy and local political priorities.

The original operational policy for the project included clear guidelines regarding responsibilities for the performance of care management. In particular, the devices employed were:

- individual user budget ceilings (set at two-thirds of the average cost of hospital care, though with scope for exceptions);
- a service 'menu' with (shadow) price information;
- service-level coordination of resources (such as unit costs for housing inputs);
- a team of care managers with health and social services backgrounds; and
- limited caseloads of around twenty to reflect demanding care management responsibilities.

The infrastructure provided administrative and professional checks and balances, as well as mechanisms for user involvement. It included a charter of user rights, an operational policy for staff responsibilities, service and support contracts with users, and a protected role for individual service planning coordination to inform service design and development. Using today's terminology, it combined lead agency, social entrepreneurship and single care manager arrangements (DH/SSI, 1991a).

The Maidstone service is now fully integrated into Kent's mainstream care management provision, with user contact and formal reviews less frequent than before. After holistic assessment, care managers arrange and purchase services such as housing and staff support from a range of agencies, including the voluntary and private sectors. (The pilot project had helped to establish a housing association which is now one of the biggest not-for-profit providers of housing and staff support for people with learning disabilities in the county.) Care management in Kent is an integral part of the authority's market-oriented commissioning function and is the most devolved level at which purchasing decisions are made.

Each geographical division in the county has separate care management budgets for the elderly and disability teams. Care managers for disability have caseloads comprising people with both physical and learning disabilities, separated into more and less complex cases, totalling in excess of fifty users. Work is still under way on integrating the ISP and service cost information systems needed for the direct purchasing of a full range of services (Figure 9.1). This emphasises the importance of developing the necessary care management information systems in parallel to reorganisation or the introduction of new care management arrangements. The move towards mixed caseloads in respect of complexity of need and user group could help reduce the traditional labelling of users and the service and resource boundaries currently found between the user groups in community care, when reinforced by holistic assessment.

The operation of care management

The implementation of assessment and care management by social services departments was delayed until April 1993, giving time for some reflection and consolidation. Care management is one of the cornerstones of the government's community care reforms, and there has been a series of guidance documents and numerous articles in the professional journals and books debating the merits of alternative care management arrangements (including none at all). From an accumulating body of knowledge about the development of care-managed services, we might expect converging practice, with new systems evolving in the light of experience and cross-fertilisation between authorities. It is perhaps too early, however, to review the performance and

Figure 9.1
Care management in Kent's organisational structure

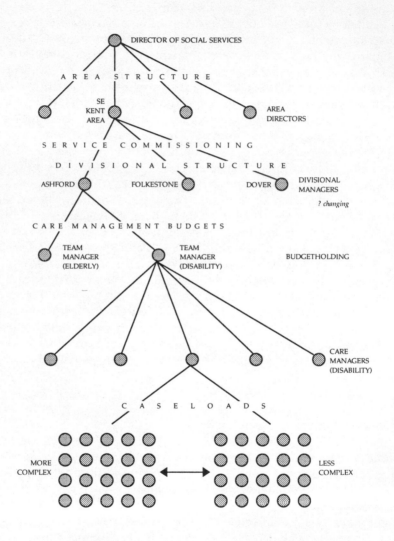

effectiveness of different approaches and designs as there are also forces working against common practice or minimum standards. The permissive nature of the policy guidance material presented models and options rather than prescriptions. The proliferation of pilot experiments and designs illustrates the sheer organisational diversity of care management. Can the twelve services help us make sense of this variety?

One of the main challenges for care management is to respond to user needs within available individual, team or agency budgets. In three of the twelve areas, the emerging care management systems are based on *devolved budgets*, in some cases because they are considered to reinforce the professional advocacy role. In some areas they were also seen to provide opportunities for substituting inappropriate services and evolving brokerage arrangements, creating openings for user empowerment (Cambridge, 1992b).

Although most care managers were also professional advocates, it was recognised that service users needed to be involved in decisions about their lives and services. As we described in Chapter 4, many accommodation facilities had promoted *user involvement*, and this can also be formalised in operational policies or charters which stipulate rights and responsibilities through contracts with care managers. However, there was evidence from some of the twelve areas that the inclusion of financial dimensions and imperatives created disincentives for user consultation and involvement.

Some aspects of care management arrangements warrant particular mention.

Continuity of user-care manager relationships can help foster user involvement, and continuity is vital for developing the coherent perspectives necessary for ISP. But continuity can be difficult to maintain when users move between services or systems, even though shared information and planning systems can help limit the damage. In some places, such as Camden and Islington, overlapping but non-integrated care management systems were emerging. Among the lessons from the twelve projects is the need for local clarity and agreement on the boundaries for care management responsibility within and between agencies and across the commissioning-purchasing divide.

The frequency and type of *contact between users and care managers* partly determine the nature of the relationship and the knowledge held by the care manager about individual needs, abilities and aspirations. In hierarchical systems, where team managers, care managers and keyworkers liaise for case review, frequency of user contact for professionals may vary according to factors such as the resource implications of ISP and the service agenda. Reviews at least every six months were found to be necessary for most people with long-term support needs. The fact that some services were reducing the frequency of ISP and reviews suggests that users may have reached the perceived ceiling of ability within the scope of the service model, available resources or competences of staff.

The level of responsibility for purchasing, budgetary autonomy, service specification and coordination, user continuity and client contact all largely depend on *caseload size*. Most care management experiments limit caseloads to between fifteen and twenty users to provide space for the more intensive tasks of care management or the administrative work required for devolved authority. In the twelve areas, this size caseload was not uncommon, although it became a luxury in some areas, for example, as we have seen in Kent. Here the authority had begun to move towards a more generic approach to organising community care, and it will be interesting to watch such developments in the future.

It proved important to be clear how *keyworking* and care management roles were connected or separated, unless the latter was based on an enhanced keyworking model. In some instances, such as for people living in ordinary housing, keyworkers adopted a monitoring and linking role within care management, holding responsibility for implementing training or individual care planning, advocating on the user's behalf and negotiating access to agreed services.

Some arrangements defined who was responsible for specific parts of the care management process. With *shared* core task arrangements — found in three of the study localities — different specialists or professionals, sometimes from different agencies, were allocated responsibility for the different core tasks, such as assessment or leading ISP. Projects where care management tasks were shared found that someone was needed to oversee liaison and coordination. Integrated and accessible record systems were also essential, along with clear accountability. Accountability was sometimes split between different providing services if not allocated to the purchasing or enabling authority.

Liaison and coordination were imperatives for the growing number of *care management teams* for people with learning disabilities, with each team member having a caseload, but with decisions about intake, allocation (including specialist inputs) and case closure taken by the team as a whole. These teams worked well, especially if they held a range of disciplines and skills. Having a mix of specialisms on care management teams meant that key resources were more immediately accessible. Speech therapy, occupational therapy and social work inputs proved particularly valuable when integrated in a multi-disciplinary care management team, helping to bridge agency and inter-disciplinary divides. Some of these teams evolved from the more conventional community learning disability team model and in areas like Camden specialist teams were emerging in the field of challenging behaviour (Emerson et al., 1993).

Joint health and social services teams proved especially valuable for work in hospital resettlement and rehabilitation. Some care managers retained separate line management and accountability (with service condition differentials a problem — see Chapter 5), or reported to a joint management committee.

Similar care management teams are within the scope of community care, particularly where there are long-term support needs or where public service agencies wish to reinforce a user-focused monitoring role or develop joint commissioning or purchasing arrangements.

With the *separation of purchasing from providing*, services had to decide on which side of the fence keyworkers and care managers should sit. Care managers with budgets tended to be seen as secondary purchasers. While there were conflicts of interest and accountability, even with care managers employed by social services as a purchasing agency (as in Kent) or in-house (as in Somerset), few services explored the option of commissioning independent care management. However, some of the voluntary sector-led provision began to develop quasi-independent functions. The Cambridge project experimented with agency brokerage but found it difficult to break from a dominant public sector culture. The *location* of care management was another dimension which exercised some of the original projects. In situ location (in residential or day support services) — which was the model adopted in five of the areas — risked compromising professional advocacy with providing interests. Most public sector or voluntary-led residential services effectively provided facility-based 'care management' delivered by keyworkers, team leaders or house managers. Peripatetic delivery offered a partial answer, but essential links needed to be constructed with users and workers responsible for the component parts of care packages, and management walls needed to be built between care management, residential service management and central administration.

These dimensions are not mutually exclusive and their combination will help to determine how effective and robust care management proves to be in the 1990s. With the general (as opposed to pilot) use of care management, we are witnessing a big natural experiment with little certainty about user outcomes or costs. Success will depend on how well the new arrangements are tailored to local circumstances and priorities, as well as being dependent on organisational and individual competences.

New wine, old bottles?

The Maidstone and Somerset care management arrangements were described in this and earlier chapters. They provide examples of developments in the micro-organisation of community care, although, as we have noted before, every one of the original Care in the Community projects introduced highly rationalised forms of care management. Some projects were less than adventurous, being constrained by vested interests prone to institutional risk-aversion or without the management, financial resources or competences necessary for developing such arrangements. If care management is to be expected in part or in total from providers, then commissioning agencies will need to share their specialist financial and administrative skills. Along with training and information management responsibilities, care management may need to be carefully specified and costed in contracts.

Care management will have to be concerned as much with the links between costs and outcomes as with matching resources to needs. A clear view of the former helps facilitate the monitoring of service quality and the review of service performance needed for arranging and purchasing community care services. But there are unanswered questions, such as who should hold such information. Purchasers need the information for monitoring how effectively resources are used, and providers need it for their own financial management and quality audits. Although no best approach emerged from the services for information ownership or sharing, there were pointers to the type, level and potential use of information generated by care management. The Camden experience is an example of what can happen without proper assessment, ISP and cost information.

Most community care clients use more than one care or support service, and there is inevitably a tremendous variety of care packages. Community services will need to consider whether they aim to provide comprehensive costings of individual care packages or simply the costs as they concern the commissioning agency or residential provider. In some of the twelve areas, decisions had already been made as to likely information needs with respect to individual service utilisation and costs. Steps were being taken to meet them. In Somerset and Kent this included systems designed to inform and facilitate management and practice decision-making and service planning and commissioning, such as the inclusion of service prices, and information on service availability, needed for exercising choice and service substitution. Such information will underpin effective community care and service planning at the macro-level as much as ISP. With devolved budgets goes devolved accountability, and auditors are increasingly holding services to account.

> If we have devolved budgets of whatever size, we need proper financial information systems. Anyone putting in a devolved budget without a financial information system will be put through the shredder by the auditors. With a devolved budget you need to be able to control spending, but it needs to be more than simply a financial information system. It also needs to be a commitment accounting system, which tells you exactly how much is committed — not simply what resources have been purchased as of three months ago. Better still, a forward commitments system is needed which tells you how much of the future budget is also committed, assuming client needs remain static. Such cost and client information systems are no trivial afterthought. They will be central to making case management work (Browning, 1992, pp.42-3).

Figure 9.2 shows how such systems will need to mesh with care management and community care planning. Somerset developed parallel information

Figure 9.2
Strategic aspects of inter-agency working through care management

KENT: mixed economy (enabling) model

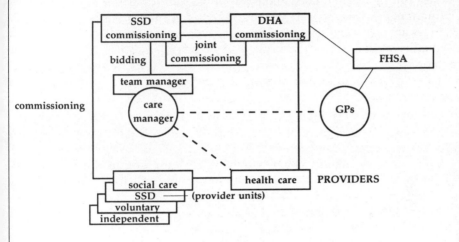

SOMERSET: lead agency (providing) model

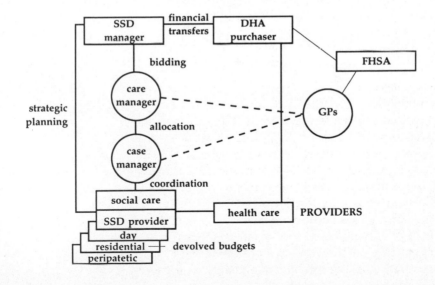

systems for service costs and service utilisation at the individual user level, and these are used to bill the health authority for services provided and to plan services around individual needs using information generated by assessment and review. Kent is developing a system devolved to care managers to allow for direct service purchasing and substitution. These systems are held and maintained by the provider in Somerset and the purchaser in Kent.

What is clear is that many authorities with a strategic approach to developing community services for people with learning disabilities will be looking to tie together information on costs and outcomes, and many large providers in whatever sector will be doing the same. We wonder whether the crisis in CSMH in Camden could have been averted had such information been available. We know that such systems can be developed and successfully operated, but know little about their organisational costs or the longer-term cost-outcome effects.

Care management is not cheap to introduce or operate, and there is always the risk that resources will be raided from other service areas to set up the necessary systems. Moreover, until a number of authorities have been operating their own care management systems for a time within the new mixed economy of community care, they will not know whether the additional organisational costs are justified by the results. The evidence from across twelve areas, however, persuades us that introducing care management in small, incremental changes may not succeed. Social services departments should not 'try to pour too much of the heady new wine into rigid old bottles' (Davies, 1992, p.32). The systems that were operating appeared effective, although, without increased user participation and control, their full potential for achieving improved and sustainable outcomes for users may never be fully realised.

10 Conclusions — Developing Community Care

The research described in this book focused on a group of people with learning disabilities who moved from long-stay hospital residence during the 1980s under the auspices of the Care in the Community demonstration programme. During the period of this research the organisation and provision of support to these people became part of mainstream community care. Because the research was undertaken in twelve different localities and involved more than 200 service users, we had the opportunity to examine a range of local practices.

As the study has shown, in the mid-1980s the twelve pilot projects were already attempting to do many of the things later demanded or encouraged by the 1990 National Health Service and Community Care Act. Each of them had carefully planned the development of community support to replace some hospital provision. The three years of protected funding from central government allowed key services to be set in place. Service delivery was coordinated (albeit sometimes imperfectly) via care management and in response to user needs. Joint working and service management between health authorities and social services departments had been introduced in many areas, some NHS responsibilities had been transferred to local government and some joint commissioning had effectively been introduced. Service commissioning often resulted in purchases from the voluntary sector and, less often, the private sector.

One of the consequences of these activities was a set of community care services of good quality according to the widely-accepted criteria of normalisation. Most community care arrangements were generally described in favourable terms by users. Since leaving hospital, individual changes in skills, behaviour, morale, social networks and participation in community living were generally positive and sometimes quite marked. Not surprisingly, only a small number of people had achieved anything approaching independent living. For most of those who had, formal services still played vital support and monitoring roles. This latter finding reflects the longer-term pattern of service provision necessary for many people with learning disabilities. Those people with greatest support needs are unlikely ever to achieve independent living.

Services for most people were coordinated by care managers in consultation with users. However, in most of the twelve areas care management was still struggling to link individual service planning information with good data on services and costs. For example, we found that the link had been achieved at a relatively early stage in Somerset, was developing by the end of the study in Maidstone, but had not yet developed in Camden and some other areas. In Somerset, individual service planning was informed by an awareness of service costs and itself informed service planning at the macro-level. Kent was in the process of developing information links between care management and service commissioning, and the financial crisis in Camden emphasised the importance of having up-to-date cost information for each individual user. These needs become increasingly urgent with the greater mixing of the economy of community care. Social services departments will have to take lead responsibility for developing and implementing information systems which will span the sectors and range of providers.

Facilitating a mixed economy of care can prove difficult. The Cambridge service, for example, tried to establish a small quasi-independent, not-for-profit assessment agency brokerage model, but found the political, legal and organisational hurdles too difficult to overcome. Incentives and opportunities need to be provided to and by local authorities for developing such organisational experiments and diversity. We witnessed very different interpretations of the enabling role, ranging from lead provision and partnerships with large voluntary providers to block purchasing from a wide range of providers across different sectors through care management.

We found evidence of both the adaptation of existing management structures and the introduction of radically new arrangements. Integral to both adaptation and innovation was the development of new or redefined functions such as commissioning and care management. In contrast, we saw few innovations in the development of checks and balances for increasingly autonomous and devolved authority, particularly relating to users' interests. With services moving away from public provision we saw growing gaps in accountability. The rationale for arm's-length inspection and regulation needs to be applied to service performance more generally. There are also questions about the extent to which contracts or care management can safeguard the interests of users and clarify accountability. Partnership and cooperation between purchasers and providers, or between different providers, can exclude users and result in new types of monopoly or unresponsive provision. We saw more choice for purchasers resulting in increasing provider fragmentation and wasteful duplication. While contracts helped define responsibilities, we also began to see the 'short-termism', instability and confrontation sometimes accompanying the contract culture, as well as little understanding of the transactions costs of contracting (Wistow et al., 1994).

Community services need both ongoing energy and enthusiasm and continued resources to maintain and extend improvements in user welfare. Yet the development of care management as a way to achieve the better targeting of resources, along with management information systems, could lead to two-tier services being raided from direct provision. Not every care management system is likely to perform well.

Résumé

From our involvement with the twelve services included in the evaluation, we know of no reasonable basis on which to challenge the policy of care in the community for people with learning disabilities who would otherwise be long-term hospital residents. In fact, most people with learning disabilities are demonstrably better off living in the community than in hospital, over both the short and long term. For most people who have lived for long periods in hospital, a number of self-care and life skills can improve significantly after the move to the community and can be maintained in the longer term. This applies similarly to a range of key welfare dimensions. People are happier in the community than in hospital, and integration into the community continues over time, along with the maintenance and development of wider social networks and more meaningful social contacts. Physical aspects of people's homes are 'more ordinary' and remain of better quality than those of the hospitals they left behind. There is also evidence of slightly more choice over living environments and support networks in the longer term.

Of course, not everyone is better off and not all services achieved the same improvements in user outcomes. A few people said they wanted to return to hospital, although those in hospital did not want to remain there. New placements have been found for some people who experienced a preference for more congregate living, just as some people have been helped to move to more independent living. Generally, however, it is not easy for people to graduate from one type of community accommodation to another as their needs change. No single policy, practice or philosophy of care suits *everyone*, but ordinary life in the community has benefited the majority of people participating in this study.

Beyond quality of life outcomes and individual abilities lies the central issue of human rights. Everyone should have the right to develop their potential and to experience life to the fullest. This includes both good and bad experiences. Without such opportunities, personal development is restricted, the ability to make informed choice is limited, and opportunities for community participation and citizenship are denied. Ordinary, everyday experiences are harder to achieve in hospital than in community settings, although we would not deny that we found some community accommodation which was some distance short of ideal in terms of quality, scale or institutional regime. Just as there are good and bad hospitals, so there are good and bad community services. The continuing economic marginalisation of service users through lack of employment and reliance on state benefits militate against economic empowerment as much as the organisational characteristics of services.

Five years on, we found that community care remained more expensive than hospital, although the allocation and distribution of costs changed, mainly in response to the further development of the provider side of the mixed economy of care. Thus, the significantly better outcomes and service opportunities in the community had been achieved at the expense of a modest increase in costs compared to hospital, although costs were no different on average after five years in the community than after one. In the fifth year after people had left hospital, they were using more health services than they had done during the first year in the community, and they were less likely to use educational services or to receive community social care support.

Organisationally, there is no doubt that the government's community care reforms raise as many questions as they answer, but this need not undermine, and apparently is not undermining, the philosophy of care in the community. Publicly-led services have demonstrated that they can organise and deliver good-quality and well-coordinated care, on their own and in partnership with housing and voluntary agencies. And service users have shown enthusiasm in seizing opportunities offered to them by a new life outside hospital.

We hope that *Five Years On* has provided a window through which to glimpse some of the emerging patterns and issues in the organisation and delivery of community care. However, it will be some time before we can view a wider perspective. The new community care landscape of the 1990s is still emerging and is likely to remain hazy and developmental for some time. In particular, we need a better understanding of the relationships between service interventions and longer-term improvements in user abilities and functioning, the latter being as much dependent on organisational skills within services as on resources alone. At the very least, however, *Five Years On* has demonstrated that the community care system has the ability, technologies and understanding to deliver better support for people with learning disabilities.

References

Audit Commission (1986) *Making a Reality of Community Care*, HMSO, London.

Audit Commission (1987) *Community Care: Developing Services for People with a Mental Handicap*, Occasional Paper No. 4, Audit Commission, London.

Audit Commission (1989) *Developing Community Care for Adults with a Mental Handicap*, Occasional Papers No. 9, Audit Commission, London.

Audit Commission (1992) *Managing the Cascade of Change*, HMSO, London.

Beecham, J.K. (1994) Collecting and estimating costs, in M.R.J. Knapp (ed.) *The Economic Evaluation of Mental Health Services*, Ashgate, Aldershot.

Beecham, J.K. and Knapp, M.R.J. (1992) Costing psychiatric options', in G. Thornicroft, C. Brewin and J. Wing (eds) *Measuring Mental Health Needs*, Oxford University Press, Oxford.

Borthwick-Duffy, S.A., Eyman, R.K. and White, J.F. (1987) Client characteristics and residential placement patterns, *American Journal of Mental Deficiency*, 92, 1, 24-30.

Brown, H. and Smith, H. (eds) (1992) *Normalisation: A Reader for the Nineties*, Routledge, London.

Browning, D. (1992) Looking to the future, in S. Onyett and P. Cambridge (eds) *Case Management: Issues in Practice*, CAPSC/PSSRU, University of Kent, Canterbury.

Cambridge, P. (1992a) Questions for case management II, in S. Onyett and P. Cambridge (eds) *Case Management: Issues in Practice*, CAPSC/PSSRU, University of Kent, Canterbury.

Cambridge, P. (1992b) Case management in community services: organisational responses, *British Journal of Social Work*, 22, 495-517.

Cantril, H. (1965) *The Pattern of Human Concerns*, Rutgers University Press, New Brunswick, New Jersey.

Challis, D.J. and Davies, B.P. (1986) *Case Management in Community Care*, Gower, Aldershot.

Cheetham, J., Fuller, R., McIvor, G. and Petch, A. (1992) *Evaluating Social Work Effectiveness*, Open University Press, Buckingham.

Conroy, J.W. and Bradley, V.J. (1985) The Pennhurst Longitudinal Study: a report of five years of research and analysis, Human Services Research Institute, Boston and Developmental Disabilities Center, Temple University, Philadelphia, Pennsylvania.

Dagnan, D., Nagel, P., Thompson, C. and Drewett, R. (1990) Family placement schemes for adults with a mental handicap in Great Britain, *Research, Policy and Planning*, 8, 2, 9-11.

Davies, B.P. (1992) Lessons for case management, in S. Onyett and P. Cambridge (eds) *Case Management: Issues in Practice*, CAPSC/PSSRU, University of Kent, Canterbury.

Department of Health/Social Services Inspectorate (1991a) *Case Management and Assessment: Managers' Guide*, HMSO, London.

Department of Health/Social Services Inspectorate (1991b) *Case Management and Assessment: Practitioners' Guide*, HMSO, London.

Emerson, E., Toogood, A., Mansell, J., Barrett, S., Bell, C., Cummings, R. and McCool, C. (1987) Challenging behaviour and community services: 1. Introduction and overview, *Mental Handicap*, 15, 4, 166-9.

Emerson, E., Cambridge, P., Forrest, J. and Mansell, J. (1993) Community support teams for people with learning disabilities, in C. Kiernan (ed.) *Research to Practice*, BILD Publications, British Institute of Learning Disabilities, Clevedon.

Feragne, M.A., Longabaugh, R. and Stevenson, J.F. (1983) The Psychosocial Functioning Inventory, *Evaluation and the Health Professions*, 6, 3, 25-48.

Griffiths, R. (1988) *Community Care: Agenda for Action*, HMSO, London.

Gunzburg, H. and Gunzburg, A. (1973) *Mental Handicap and Physical Environment: The Application of an Operational Philosophy to Planning*, Baillière Tindall, Paris.

Henke, R.O., Connolly, S.G. and Cox, J.G. (1975) Caseload management: the key to effectiveness, *Journal of Applied Rehabilitation Counselling*, 6, 4, 217-27.

Holmes, N., Shah, A. and Wing, L. (1982) The disability assessment schedule: a brief screening device for use with the mentally retarded, *Psychological Medicine*, 12, 879-90.

King, R., Raynes, N. and Tizard, J. (1971) *Patterns of Residential Care: Sociological Studies in Institutions for Handicapped Children*, Routledge and Kegan Paul, London.

King's Fund Centre (1982) *An Ordinary Life*, King's Fund, London.

Knapp, M.R.J. (1984) *The Economics of Social Care*, Macmillan, London.

Knapp, M.R.J. (1993) Background theory, in A. Netten and J.K. Beecham (eds) *Costing Community Care: Theory and Practice*, Ashgate, Aldershot.

Knapp, M.R.J. (1994) Variations and comparisons, in M.R.J. Knapp (ed.) *The Economic Evaluation of Mental Health Services*, Ashgate, Aldershot.

Knapp, M.R.J. and Wistow, G. (1993) Joint commissioning for community care, in Department of Health *Implementing Community Care: A Slice Through Time*, Department of Health/Social Services Inspectorate, London, 1993.

Knapp, M.R.J., Beecham, J., Anderson, J., Dayson, J., Leff, D., Margolius, O., O'Driscoll, C. and Wills, W. (1990) Predicting the community costs of closing psychiatric hospitals, *British Journal of Psychiatry*, 157, 661-70.

Knapp, M.R.J., Cambridge, P., Thomason, C., Beecham, J., Allen, C. and Darton, R. (1992) *Care in the Community: Challenge and Demonstration*, Ashgate, Gower.

Knapp, M.R.J., Beecham, J.K., Fenyo, A.J. and Hallam, A. (1994) Predicting costs from needs and diagnoses: community mental health care for former hospital inpatients, *British Journal of Psychiatry* 160 (Supplement), forthcoming.

O'Brien, J. (1986) *A Guide to Personal Futures Planning*, mimeo, Responsive Systems Associates, Atlanta, Georgia.

O'Brien, J. and Tyne, A. (1981) *The Principle of Normalisation: A Foundation for Effective Services*, Campaign for Mental Handicap, London.

Renshaw, J., Hampson, R., Thomason, C., Darton, R.A., Judge, K. and Knapp, M.R.J. (1988) *Care in the Community: The First Steps*, Gower, Aldershot.

Secretaries for State (1989) *Caring for People: Community Care in the Next Decade and Beyond*, Cm 849, HMSO, London.

Simons, K., Booth, T. and Booth, W. (1989) Speaking out: user studies and people with learning difficulties, *Research, Policy and Planning*, 7, 1, 9-17.

Snaith, R.P., Ahmed, S.N., Mehta, S. and Hamilton, M. (1971) Assessment of the severity of primary depressive illness, *Psychological Medicine*, 1, 143-9.

Wagner, J. (1979) *Images of Information*, Sage, Beverly Hills, California.

Ward, L. (1985) *Training for Change*, King's Fund Centre, London.

Wertheimer, A. and Greig, R. (1993) *Report on Joint Commissioning for Community Care*, National Development Team, Manchester.

Wistow, G., Knapp, M.R.J., Hardy, B. and Allen, C. (1994) *Social Care in a Mixed Economy*, Open University Press, Buckingham.

Wolfensberger, W. (1972) *The Principle of Normalization in Human Services*, National Institute on Mental Retardation, Toronto.

Wray, L. and Wieck, C. (1985) Moving persons with developmental disabilities towards less restrictive environments through case management, in K. Lakin and R. Bruinks (eds) *Strategies for Achieving Community Integration of Developmentally Disabled Citizens*, Brookes, Baltimore, Maryland.

Wykes, T. (1982) A hostel for 'new' long-stay patients: an evaluative study of a 'ward in a house', in J.K. Wing (ed.) *Psychological Medicine*, Monograph Supplement, 57-97.

Subject index

Name Index